SALT
of the
EARTH

Secrets and Stories
from a Greek Kitchen

Carolina Doriti

Photography by Manos Chatzikonstantis

Hardie Grant

QUADRILLE

This book is dedicated, with love, to my son, Apollo.

CONTENTS

Introduction

I grew up in Greece, a country full of history, and have lived most of my life in Athens, a city that wonderfully blends and balances the ancient with the modern. For me, this blend is how I experience the cuisine of this age-old culture. Its roots are ancient, its core has been preserved, yet it has harmoniously developed over the years, and I would say has been gracefully touched by the course of history, from both West and East.

I have been cooking from a very young age and food has been an integral part of my life. I experience a unique pleasure from cooking and a whole different level of pleasure from eating. I owe this joy of eating to my beloved grandfather George, who taught me so much, and I owe my love of cooking to my mother Tesi, who gave me my first cookbook as soon as I was able to read.

Cooking is a form of art, of communication, and indeed an expression of love; love is an essential ingredient in all the dishes I cook. I like food with soul, no matter where it comes from and how fast or simple it is to prepare. To me, Greek cuisine is fresh and seasonal; an ancient, wise kitchen with soul. Sustainable and resourceful, it is principally a maternal cuisine that is nutritious and comforting at the same time. It doesn't need too many elements or anything fancy, but it will certainly impress your senses and tastebuds.

Just as every ingredient and dish can be associated with a time and place in Greece's history, for me every flavour and scent is associated with a special memory in my own history. A taste of *avgolemono* instantly transports me to my grandmother's kitchen; the scent of *melomakarona* feels like my mother's hug; while *botargo* reminds me of my grandfather, with whom I always shared it.

The geographic location of a country hugely defines its cuisine, and Greece is no exception. Food is produced all over the country, even on the driest island, where you might savour the best thyme honey or the most flavourful capers, wild oregano, tiny chickpeas, fresh cheese, or the freshest seafood. Every single part of Greece is blessed with at least a couple of exceptional food products. I have had the pleasure and luck of travelling a lot around the country, researching regional cuisines: their local produce, the ingredients and techniques they use, as well as the wonderful results. Moreover, it is astonishing to me how a small country like Greece has such regional diversity in its cuisine and how each region retains its own sense of tradition – not just in the recipes themselves, but in all the associated traditions, including the way each dish is served, eaten and celebrated. It is this wonderment and intrigue that pushed me to dive deeper into Hellenic cuisine and the more I discover from the history that unravels, the prouder I feel.

By studying the cuisine and recipes of a culture, you obtain a much better understanding of the history and how different cultures exchanged their knowledge and experience through their culinary worlds; traditions acquired and passed on by the civilizations from which we evolved. I have always been fascinated by ancient history and Greek mythology – mostly concerning the anthropological and sociological side of it: how they were educated, how they used to spend their day, what their eating habits were, their religious customs and how those were connected to food and ingredients, and other such questions. I found the answers in history books and essays, in Greek mythology and in the writings of ancient masters, including Homer and Herodotus.

I believe it is our duty to treasure and preserve our culinary traditions and recipes. All of them, if we can: recipes that evolved out of need and poverty and were then forgotten; recipes that have already been preserved for centuries or altered along the way; recipes or ingredients with symbolic meanings; recipes that require time and skill. They are our history and heritage.

My passion for gastronomy is constantly alive and growing. It gives me great pleasure to share in this book the knowledge and experience of Greek cuisine and culture that I have lovingly built up. I hope that through this I can contribute to the revival of old recipes that may be lesser known but worth preserving. At the same time, I like to dig into the story of each dish, the traditions associated with it, or its symbolic meaning. I hope to transport the reader to the Greece I love so much, and to present through each recipe the different regions and islands, their local produce, folk tales and traditions.

I have chosen to divide this book into chapters that offer an ingredient-centric approach to cooking, selecting the core foods that have defined Greek cuisine for several centuries. Recipes cater for all levels of cook, for different styles of palate, flavour or dietary requirement. While I encompass all kinds of recipes, including those for meat and seafood, my main chapter ingredients are plant-based, because plant-based dishes are the true essence of the traditional Greek kitchen. Meat is there, but it would have been used in smaller amounts in order to add flavour and protein rather than be the actual star of the dish – with certain exceptions, of course, that were mostly related to special occasions.

By focusing on one main ingredient, or the source – such as the hive, or a whole plant such as the vine or olive tree – and showing the many different ways it can be used, I aim to present recipes that are accessible, sustainable and cost-efficient while also being satisfying, nutritious and, of course, delicious. Greek cuisine is shaped creatively in order to make use of everything available and I feel ultimate fulfilment when I have used all possible parts of an ingredient; this is the greatest way to honour and respect it.

Simple, flavourful, comforting, nourishing, and certainly seasonal food is what I aim for when I cook, and it's what I usually crave to eat and share with others. With this book, I invite you to explore the wonderful secrets of my own Greek kitchen, with all its history and heart-warming tales.

Kali orexi![1]

---

[1] 'bon appétit' in Greek

The Roots and Evolution of Greek Cuisine

Greek cuisine is shaped by a prodigious climate, diverse landscape and abundant natural resources. The ancient knowledge of working with the land and the sea, being in coherence with the seasons and respectful to what nature has to offer, is evident in the local gastronomy.

Gastronomy is an ancient Greek word, deriving from the words *gastir* (stomach) and *nomia* (knowledge, law), literally meaning the 'rules/law of the stomach'. Both words, *gastir* and *nomia*, have been used in the Greek language since Homer's time, but the term is actually attributed to Archestratus, the 4th century BCE Greek poet, who was possibly the first to study and write to such an extent about the pleasures of eating and the laws of appetite. In his work, *Hydipathia* or *Gastronomia*[1], the gourmet writer of antiquity wittily describes the secrets of ancient Greek gastronomy, shares full recipes, and dedicates whole chapters to wine, pulses and fish – ingredients that remain staples in present-day Greek cuisine. Athenaeus, in his book *Deipnosophistae* (*Dinner Sophists*) written in the early 3rd century CE, also provides valuable information about eating habits and particular recipes; his book describes in detail banquet conversations on food, literature and the arts.

Several other writings, including Homer's stories, Aristophanes' plays, Plato's *Symposium* and the works of Hippocrates, who preached: 'Let food be your medicine and medicine be your food', clarify ancient eating habits. Archaeological excavations have also proved invaluable, with some of the oldest findings dating to the Bronze Age Aegean Civilization[2] that brought to light not only the main ingredients that

were used, but also specialized equipment and cooking methods. We know, for instance, that the ancient Greeks made sausages, and matured cheese in caves; they grilled skewered meat (similar to today's *souvlaki*) on *krateftes*[3], and they loved *garon* (a fermented fish sauce later named 'garum' by the Romans) and served it as a condiment with almost every dish. They baked breads and pies – which in fact were a particularly popular snack in 5th century BCE Athens. We know the diet was generally based on three main ingredients: the olive, vine and cereal. Other ingredients commonly used included pulses, honey, vegetables and fruit, nuts and seeds, fish and seafood, herbs, snails, eggs, cheese, and a variety of specific meats and game, although meat in general was consumed mostly by the upper classes or on special occasions. The use of herbs was extensive, with a wide variety that included thyme, coriander (cilantro), parsley, dill, basil, marjoram, rosemary, bay, oregano and others. Apart from in cooking, herbs were also used medicinally.

Trade was a big part of the economy, bringing cultural interaction and exchange. The ancient Greeks were organized merchants and seamen who travelled a lot around the region and were consequently inspired by other great cultures such as the Assyrians, the Phoenicians (Canaanites) and the Egyptians. Several findings around the Mediterranean region, including shipwrecks, have revealed much about ancient commerce, imports and exports. Greeks imported spices and other 'exotic' goods such as aniseed from Egypt and rosinweed from Libya, and they exported olive oil, olives and wine, among other goods.

---

[1] The work survives in *Deipnosophistae*, an early 3rd-century CE work written by Athenaeus.
[2] Which includes the Minoan Civilization on Crete c. 2000–1450 BCE, the Mycenaean Civilization on mainland Greece c. 1700–1100 BCE and the Cycladic Civilization on the islands of the Cyclades c. 3200–1050 BCE.
[3] A special grilling device; the most ancient one exhibited at the museum of Akrotiri on the island of Santorini dates 1600 BCE.

Mythology provides another excellent source of information about the diet and culinary traditions of the ancient Greeks. The foundations of the diet are summarized with the three *Oenotrophae* (the 'winegrowers'), the granddaughters of God Dionysus: Elais, whose name derives from *elia*, which in Greek means olive, her sister Spermo, deriving from *sperma* which in Greek means seed, and Oeno, deriving from *oenos*, which means wine. The three sisters represent the three main ingredients of the Greek diet: olive oil, wheat and wine. This core diet endured over the centuries. Many recipes were adopted and further developed by the Romans, who were the most proficient disseminators of culinary traditions in the West.

The diet and cuisine during the Byzantine era (395–1453 CE) remained largely the same, aside from the introduction of a handful of ingredients, such as nutmeg, cinnamon, cloves, *botargo* and caviar. Valuable information can be gleaned about everyday Byzantine life from the 10th century CE dictionary titled *Souda*, and extensive and remarkable literary research on the specific subject has been done by Sir Richard Dalby, among others. This research highlights that anise-infused spirits (the predecessors of what was later named ouzo) were prepared and offered as aperitifs, and exported throughout the Mediterranean; baking was considered a prestigious occupation for the Byzantines, while desserts gradually became more elaborate and complex, with an extensive use of milk in certain recipes, such as rice puddings and cream pies (like *galaktoboureko* and *bougatsa*); fruit preserves and compotes were also particularly popular at the time. Still, the principal ingredients remained the same: olive oil, wine, grains, nuts and seeds, fruit and honey.

Byzantine culture was greatly affected by the new religion of Christianity. A lot of Greek and Roman practices – including some eating habits – were considered pagan and were either eliminated (for instance the use of blood in food like sausages) or incorporated gradually until 'Christianized' and approved. The new religion encouraged people to be humble and follow a simple lifestyle and diet. Animal-derived foods were eaten less as more Lent periods were inserted into the calendar; thus vegetarianism was enforced. This was the beginning of what became known as the 'Greek Monastery Cuisine' – a highly plant-based diet that occasionally included fish and seafood.

The complex history of Greece and its geographic location, that was for years unstable, have proven invaluable to the formation of a national cuisine: constant occupations and cultural interactions have resulted in an astonishing regional culinary diversity, despite the country's small size. During the rule of the Franks and the Venetians after the Fourth Crusade (1204), a number of mostly French, Venetian and Genoise states were established in regions of the fallen Byzantine Empire, leaving their most evident marks particularly on the islands, as well as in parts of the Peloponnese. With the arrival of the Ottomans, an Eastern, Asiatic flair was added to certain dishes. While adopting culinary traditions of the different cultures they occupied, the Ottomans incorporated those of great civilizations such as the Persians and the Arabs; the rich Byzantine culinary traditions lived on and became further enriched by these Eastern elements. Coffee and sugar gradually made their entry, butter was used more, desserts became more luscious, and the use of spices was further ingrained. With the fall of the Ottoman Empire, these legendary cuisines were gradually introduced via the exchange of populations between Greece and Turkey at different times in history, particularly between 1922 and 1957. Other influences came from parts of Anatolia and from the Pontos region of the Black Sea. The deportation of Greeks and persecuted Armenians, who had been settled in Asia Minor for thousands of years, and their resulting arrival in Greece had enormous culinary influence and enriched the cuisine in astonishing ways.

When the modern Greek state was established after the Greek War of Independence in 1821, Athens was in a poor condition in terms of both infrastructure and identity. Due to its glorious past, a significant number of people, including politicians, archaeologists, historians, architects, scholars, businessmen, from both within and outside Greece, all worked together to re-establish the city, its cultural heritage, and historic significance in the foundations of Western Civilization. The cuisine of Athens gradually became a mix of the different regional cuisines of the people who started moving into the city.

During the early 1930s, Nikolaos Tselementes, a Greek chef from the island of Sifnos who grew up in Athens and had spent time in Europe and the US, published a famous cookbook that for the first time redefined and modernized Greek cuisine. He fused mostly French-inspired elements (which were fashionable at the time) into more rustic Greek classics, and he artfully balanced Eastern and Western features in popular recipes. Bechamel sauce made its entry into the Greek kitchen in staple dishes such as *moussaka* and *pastitsio*, French pastry-making techniques were incorporated, and mayonnaise became a common ingredient in this more modern and sophisticated

style of cooking, which was officially named 'Urban Greek Cuisine'. It was further developed and enriched after World War II, and particularly during the 1950s and 60s, mostly in the larger cities such as Athens and Thessaloniki.

In 1948, the Rockefeller Foundation conducted a study on the suffering post-war population of Crete. To their astonishment, the studies showed that the locals, despite facing financial and other difficulties, were surprisingly healthy. Allbaugh et al. describe the diet of the Cretans at the time as rich in 'olives, cereal grains, pulses, wild greens and herbs, and fruits' with 'limited quantities of goat meat and milk, game, and fish' and 'swimming in olive oil'.[4] The first published mention of the term 'Mediterranean diet' appeared in 1953 and a further study on the health benefits of the specific diet was followed with the research known as the Seven Countries Study, conceived and led by Ancel Keys. In 2010, UNESCO affirmed that the diet of the countries overlooking the Mediterranean Basin represented 'a cultural heritage of humanity'.

In terms of 'fast food', the global shift in the 1980s gradually reached Greece as well, particularly during the 1990s, when I was a teenager. International fast-food chains started opening up in the big cities and ready-made frozen or processed food became a trend, mostly in order to ease the lives of working women, whose numbers were constantly increasing and thriving. Thankfully the trend proved temporary in Greece, with few of the large fast-food chains remaining open. Home-cooked food is rooted in the heart of every Greek and our national street food *souvlaki* (in its different forms) has remained people's number one choice for ages, as have the pies like *spanakopita*.

[4] Allbaugh, L.G. 'Crete: A Case Study of an Underdeveloped Area'. Princeton, New Jersey; Princeton University Press; 1953.

Over the last twenty years or so, there has been a big turn towards tradition, regional cooking and local, artisanal products. The simplicity of the traditional cuisine, preserved over the years, has been re-evaluated and further appreciated for its health benefits, simplicity and respect for the ingredients that define it. Greek chefs are doing a great job, making their mark on the global culinary scene, winning awards for their creativity, and being motivated and inspired by the high-quality ingredients produced around the country. From high-end restaurants to simple *tavernas*, Greek cuisine is thriving, and seeing this fills me with so much pride. This book is my offering to the history and heritage of Greek cuisine and culture, and I hope it represents one more step into the widening circle of culinary secrets, so that even more people can learn, share and enjoy the wonderment of what passionate home cooks and chefs in Greece have been privy to and revelling in for generations.

Notes on the Recipes

All **citrus** should be unwaxed, especially if using the zest or peel.

All **eggs** should be free-range or organic.

In Greece, **tomatoes** are traditionally grated when used in home-style cooked dishes. After washing, grate the tomatoes whole until only the skin is left in your hand. Alternatively, you can blanch them for a couple of minutes to remove the skin, then chop or pulse them in a blender. If fresh ripe tomatoes are not available, I recommend using good-quality canned instead, along with some warm water.

While inviting you to share in my passion for Greek cuisine, I would love to show you around the farmers' markets on the mainland and islands where I buy the best **seasonal produce**; sadly I cannot do that. However, suitable ingredients are available online (see page 254) for those who don't have ready suppliers in their locality.

OLIVE

The Tree of Eternity

Excavation findings show that the olive tree has been growing on this side of the world for over 50,000 years.[1] According to Greek mythology, the first olive tree was planted on the Acropolis hill of Athens – a gift of Goddess Athena to the city and its people. It was due to this gift that the goddess of wisdom won the mythic contest over Poseidon, acquiring her title as the city's patron, giving it her name, and teaching the Athenians the precious art of producing olive oil.

Records show that the wild olive tree probably originated on the Mediterranean coast of Syria and Palestine. It was brought to Greece by the Phoenicians, and the Greeks were the first to cultivate and introduce it to Europe. Through the use and export of its products, great ancient civilizations gained power and prosperity. The tree became deeply connected to Greek culture and landscape, becoming a symbol of many important virtues and meanings, such as peace and victory, knowledge and wisdom, wealth and abundance, health and beauty, power and hope. Such was its importance in the ancient world that special laws were written to protect the trees. The winners of the Panathenaic Games (athletic

competitions and cultural events that took place in ancient Athens every four years) were granted a significant amount of olive oil, while the winner of the Olympic Games was crowned with a *kotinos* (an olive leaf wreath) made from the olive tree that grew outside the temple of Zeus in Olympia. Olive oil was one of the main gifts offered to the gods and Athenian coins depicted olive trees, branches, leaves or olive leaf wreaths.

The tree ages beautifully. The trunk grows large, acquiring sculpture-like shapes, and several ancient trees survive across Greece – even in the centre of Athens. The oldest olive tree in the world, which still bears olives, is said to be on Crete. The exact age of the tree cannot be determined but it is estimated as being between 3,000 and 5,000 years old.

Over centuries, the olive tree has been used in every possible way, from the leaves to the stone (pit) and the roots. The olives are consumed as fruit, the higher quality oil is used in food, with the lower qualities in soap-making and cosmetics or oil lamps. The roots, trunk and leaves are used medicinally, as is the oil. The stones and wood are used for heating, and the wood also for carving; this whole use of the olive tree

---

[1] According to findings on the volcanic islands of Nisyros and Santorini.

has continued uninterrupted. Much of the tree's symbolic meaning was adopted by the Greek Orthodox Church, with olive oil becoming a symbol of life, present in all ritualistic traditions and practices including birth, baptism, marriage and death.

Liquid Gold

The 'juice' of the olives (*Olea europaea*) became the foundation of Greek and other Mediterranean diets. Homer referred to it as 'liquid gold' while Hippocrates called it the 'great healer'. Greece is literally covered in olive trees, and both olives and olive oil are produced right across the country, with over 30 native varieties[2].

Historically, the use of olive oil was never limited to consumption. From ancient times, it was used to produce cleansing products, aromatic oils and other cosmetics. The ancient Greek athletes anointed their bodies with olive oil not just to rehydrate and make their bodies shine, but also to protect their muscles and prevent injuries. Even contemporary cosmetic- and soap-making greatly relies on the use of olive oil, while the Greek folk tradition is full of remedies using olive oil in face and hair masks, eye treatment, nail care, or dermatological treatments.

The olive harvest begins in late autumn and ends in December, depending on region and variety. The best oil is made from the early harvest, as these olives are packed with the most nutrients. Unlike wine, olive oil doesn't age well and is best consumed fresh (within a year of production, but ideally within six months) and raw/uncooked for maximum benefit. The varieties used for oil usually differ from the varieties used for table olives; it is possible to produce olive oil from

a table olive variety, and vice versa, but the quality will not be as high. However, there are a few exceptions to this, such as the *manaki* variety, which makes an excellent mild-flavoured olive oil as well as very popular round-shaped table olives. Smaller olives generally give better quality oil, with the larger and more meaty types best for eating.

To preserve its high nutritional profile, flavour and aroma, olive oil should be cold pressed. The colour does not necessarily determine an oil's quality, and has more to do with the levels of chlorophyl; its quality is determined by its flavour, aroma and level of acidity. Extra virgin olive oil has an acidity lower or equal to 0.8 degrees, while the acidity in virgin olive oil is below 2 degrees. If the acidity of an olive oil exceeds 2 degrees, then this is classified as refined oil and is much poorer in quality and nutrients, such as olive-pomace oil. It also has a lower smoke point; the lower the acidity, the higher the smoke point, meaning that lower-quality olive oils have rather low smoke points. Greece produces high-quality olive oil, with around 80 per cent of the annual production rated as extra virgin. When an olive oil is spicy and slightly burns your throat when you swallow, it indicates a high phenolic oil (containing high levels of polyphenol compounds, which are high in antioxidants and other healing properties) and is a good sign!

When I cook, I only use extra virgin olive oil. It is wrong to think that you cannot cook with olive oil, as it has a temperature tolerance of around 180–200°C (350–400°F), depending on the quality and freshness; so as long as you avoid very high temperatures, it's best to use olive oil over any other cooking oil. In salads or to finish off a dish – always off the heat

---

[2] It is hard to accurately determine the varieties of olives because similar varieties are often named differently when cultivated in different regions and the only accurate way of determining the actual number is to conduct DNA tests. This has not been done yet in Greece.

– I use high phenolic extra virgin or early harvest olive oils. As far as flavour and aroma are concerned, I treat olive oil as I do wine. The different varieties bring out different aromas and flavours in a dish and pair with specific foods.

Olive oil is present in most Greek recipes one way or another, including many desserts. A good olive oil can create wonders, as is evident when you try it on something very simple such as drizzled on a sliced tomato, on boiled greens or in traditional recipes featured in this chapter that are classed as *ladera* (see page 48).

Storing olive oil correctly is very important to retain its nutritional value. It is UV and heat sensitive, so is best kept in dark glass bottles in a cool, dark place. It should be well sealed because, like wine, it can oxidize.

The Superfruit

The first documented consumption of olives can be traced to Greece, and specifically Crete, during the early period of Minoan civilization, around 3,500 BCE. They would have been eaten straight from the tree, or picked overripe from the ground; a very ripe olive turns dark and wrinkly, and is far less bitter. Those that mature on the tree are called *throubes*, while the ones that fall on the ground are called *hamades* ('hamo' meaning down). *Throubes* are considered among the healthiest type of olives as they require nothing more to cure and preserve than a bit of sea salt.

The ancient Greeks consumed many types of table olives and were the first to cure and export them. Most types require soaking in changes of water or salt water before they are ready to cure and herbs such as fennel, oregano and thyme were added to those preserved in brine. Garlic, honey and *oxymeli* (a mix of vinegar and honey that was also recommended by Hippocrates) were also often added. They also prepared an olive paste from black olives mixed with oil, vinegar and herbs, called *epityron* – similar to tapenade – which was eaten alongside cheese.

There are plenty of varieties of eating olives in Greece, often named after their region or town of origin such as Kalamata, Amfissis, Chalkidikis or Agriniou. Among my favourite olives are *damaskinoelies*, or prune olives; very large and often oven-dried. Olives are also sometimes named after the method of preparation, such as *throubes* and *tsakistes* (meaning 'cracked').

Olives may be green or pale brown, turning darker as they mature, and are cured at all stages of ripeness – from green, to medium, mature, to very ripe/black and wrinkled. They are packed with antioxidants and healthy fats, are a good source of vitamin E, iron, copper, calcium, and oleic acid – a monounsaturated fatty acid with numerous health benefits. Their nutritional value is aligned with that of olive oil and sometimes even higher, but this does depend on the way they have been cured. In Greece olives are usually consumed on a daily basis – as a snack, in salads, sandwiches, pies and other preparations. Olives are also made into jam and as a sweet – preserved whole in a thick syrup.

The Healing Tree

As well as the prominence of olive oil and olives in the Greek diet, and their multiple benefits to wellbeing, the olive tree has, for centuries, been used for healing purposes. The ancient Greeks were the first to record the tree's medicinal value and use of the different parts of the plant. Hippocrates prescribes olive oil for over 60 medical problems, including the relief of skin and stomach problems, muscle pains, ulcers, nausea, and during childbirth, poisoning and fever. Modern medical research into oils with a high phenolic index has found them to be beneficial against heart disease, diabetes, high cholesterol, Alzheimer's, obesity, and even cancer.

The leaves of the olive tree, which have the highest level of oleuropein[3] of all the parts of the tree, were used extensively in ancient and folk medicine, and have been used in detoxing practices as well as alternative methods for fighting cancer. The leaves are sold dried to use for tea, but several curing methods call for chewing or juicing fresh leaves. The most important thing is to make sure they are free from pesticides. Packaged olive leaves are the safest choice for those who have no access to an organic olive grove.

---

[3] A type of phenolic compound that is traced in olive skin and seed – but most of all the leaves – which has been proved to be very beneficial for the health, with strong anti-inflammatory, cardioprotective and neuroprotective functions.

'Monastery-style' aubergine salad with black olives and sun-dried tomatoes

This is one of the most popular meze dishes in Greece, with many regional variations. It falls into the category known as *alifes*, or spreads, which includes well-known spreadable dips. A favourite take on the aubergine salad is the monastery version, which is simple and vegan. Over the years, Greek monasteries and nunneries have developed their own style of cuisine, with recipes that are primarily plant-based, healthy and easy to make, with olive oil playing a central role, although on very strict Lent days like Good Friday, all pleasures are forbidden – including olive oil.

This is served as a sharing plate, but it can also be used in sandwiches or on bruschetta, or even mixed with pasta for a quick meal. I mostly enjoy eating this slightly warm, as a side to smoked or grilled fish – particularly oily fish like mackerel, sardines and anchovies.

The secret here lies in the smoky effect from cooking the aubergine; you can either grill them whole on a barbecue (grill) or directly on an open flame. However, if you don't have access to an open flame or barbecue, the easiest way is to place them under the grill (broiler) and cook them whole in the oven, as directed here. Whichever method you choose, it's best to first pierce them (and the peppers) all around with a fork or toothpick, which will prevent them from exploding. It's also important to let the aubergine drain well before you chop or cream it. If the final result is too loose, you can always mix in a couple of teaspoons of breadcrumbs, but if you allow it to drain well, that will not be necessary.

SERVES 4–6 AS A SHARING PLATE

4 medium aubergines (eggplants), about 900g (2lb) in total
1 red (bell) pepper
1 large garlic clove, roughly chopped
½ small red onion (about 70g/2½oz), roughly chopped
50g (2oz) pitted Kalamata olives, chopped
30g (1oz) sun-dried tomatoes, roughly chopped
1 tsp dried oregano
2 tbsp roughly chopped parsley
1½ tbsp balsamic vinegar
50ml (2fl oz) extra virgin olive oil
Sea salt and freshly ground black pepper

Preheat the grill (broiler) to 200°C/400°F/gas mark 6. (Alternatively, you can cook them on a barbecue/grill or over an open flame.)

Place the aubergines (eggplants) and (bell) pepper on a baking tray and grill (broil) for 30–35 minutes, turning them regularly, until slightly charred, soft and wrinkly.

Remove and let cool for 10–15 minutes.

Make a slit in the aubergines and, with a spoon, scoop out all the insides. Discard the big seeds and transfer the flesh to a fine sieve set over a bowl. Sprinkle with salt and leave to drain for 10–15 minutes.

Peel the skin off the pepper, remove the stem and seeds and chop the flesh. Set aside.

Chop half the drained aubergine and place the remaining half in a food processor with the garlic; pulse until smooth. Tip the creamed aubergine into the bowl with the chopped aubergine. Mix in the chopped pepper, onion, olives, sun-dried tomatoes, oregano, parsley and balsamic vinegar. Gradually drizzle in the olive oil while stirring fast with a fork. Season with salt and black pepper to taste.

Eliopsomo, olive bread with herbs (two ways)

The staple foods of the ancient Greeks included bread, cheese and olives. Although there were bakeries in the big city centres, bread was mostly home baked and consumed on a daily basis. Everyday bread was typically made of barley and often salt and herbs, such as fennel and mint, were added to the dough for more flavour. The most common barley bread was called *maza* (mass) and it was shaped into a kind of patty. The ancient Greek breakfast, *akratisma*, was simply bread, often *maza*, dunked in wine and accompanied by olives and figs.

There are several Greek recipes for olive bread. This recipe is by far my favourite. I use the olives as a filling and I mix them with herbs for more flavour and aroma. I give two options for fillings, one with green olives and the other with black. Feel free to play with different herbs, or mix different olives together.

MAKES 6 BUNS
35g (1¼oz) fresh yeast
650ml (22fl oz) lukewarm water
1 tsp sugar
1kg (2lb 3oz) strong white bread flour, plus extra if needed
2 tbsp olive oil, plus extra for greasing
1 tbsp fine sea salt
2–3 tbsp sesame seeds to sprinkle on top (optional)

FOR THE BLACK OLIVE AND OREGANO FILLING
4 tbsp coarsely chopped pitted Kalamata olives
1 tsp dried oregano

FOR THE GREEN OLIVE AND FENNEL FILLING
4 tbsp coarsely chopped pitted green olives
1 tbsp roughly chopped fennel fronds or dill

Dissolve the yeast in 150ml (5fl oz) of the warm water in a medium bowl. Mix in the sugar and 2 tablespoons of the flour and let it stand for 20–30 minutes until frothy and risen.

Sift the remaining flour into a large bowl. Form a well in the centre and pour in the olive oil, salt and the yeast mixture.

Start kneading by hand, slowly adding the remaining water until all is incorporated. Fold and knead gently. The dough should be elastic and soft but not sticky (if necessary, add a bit more flour).

Grease the bowl with a little olive oil, form the dough into a ball and place in the bowl. Cover with a dish towel and let stand for 2 hours until doubled in size.

Prepare your olive fillings by mixing the chopped olives with the herbs.

Divide the dough into six equal-sized balls, each weighing around 300g (10½oz). Stretch each ball out and add about 1–1½ tablespoons of filling to the centre. Stuff three of them with the black olive and three with the green olive mixture. Pull the dough around the filling to form a ball again and pinch it tightly on the base to seal.

Place the buns seal side down on a baking tray lined with baking parchment, leaving space between them. Cover with a dish towel and let rise for another 30 minutes. Meanwhile, preheat the oven to 210°C/190°C fan/410°F/gas mark 6½.

Sprinkle the risen buns with sesame seeds, if desired, then bake for 35 minutes until cooked and golden. Remove from the oven and place on a wire rack to rest for 15–20 minutes before cutting.

Prawn *saganaki* with feta and olives

Although there are several variations of this popular dish, it is most commonly prepared in a tomato sauce with melting crumbled feta[1]. Its name derives from the pan in which it is traditionally cooked, which is called 'sagani' or 'saganaki' (a diminutive for *sagani*), a round and shallow pan with two small handles that can be used both on the stovetop and in the oven. Other common recipes prepared in a saganaki pan and named after it include ingredients such as mussels and cheese.

This is a very fast dish to prepare and a very rewarding one. If you don't have ouzo[2], you can use brandy or white wine instead. Ideally, use whole prawns (shrimp) for this as the heads add the best flavour. I love serving it straight from the pan with warm, crusty bread to dunk into the delicious sauce. This recipe can also be used as a sauce to mix with pasta, or served over a bowl of rice or quinoa. But first try it plain and, most importantly, share it!

SERVES 4 AS A SHARING PLATE
300g (10½oz) shell-on medium prawns
  (shrimp), fresh or frozen (defrosted
  if frozen)
2 tbsp olive oil
1 medium onion, chopped
2 garlic cloves, sliced into thin slivers
2 bay leaves
1–2 sprigs of thyme
150ml (5fl oz) ouzo
200g (7oz) teardrop or cherry tomatoes,
  halved
270g (10oz) tomato passata (sieved
  tomatoes)
50ml (2fl oz) warm water
70g (2½oz) Kalamata olives, pitted
60g (2oz) feta, crumbled
Sea salt and freshly ground black pepper
Extra virgin olive oil, to serve

Peel and clean/devein the prawns (shrimp), keeping their heads and tails in place. Season with a little salt and pepper and set aside.

Place a large, ovenproof pan over a medium heat, heat half the olive oil and sauté the prawns for 1–2 minutes just until they change colour. Transfer to a plate.

In the same pan, heat the remaining oil and sauté the onion until soft and glossy. Add the garlic, bay leaves and thyme, stir for another minute, then pour in the ouzo. Give it a couple of minutes to infuse, then add the halved tomatoes, stir and pour in the passata and warm water. Season with a little salt (keep in mind that you'll be adding feta and olives which are salty) and plenty of pepper, lower the heat to medium and let it cook for 5–8 minutes until the sauce thickens.

Meanwhile, preheat the oven to 210°C/190°C fan/410°F/gas mark 6½.

Return the prawns to the pan, add the olives and sprinkle the crumbled feta on top. Transfer the pan to the oven and cook for another 15 minutes, or until the feta starts melting. Remove from the oven, drizzle with a little extra virgin olive oil and serve immediately.

---

[1] Without doubt the best known, most widespread and versatile of Greek cheeses, a PDO product and the star of myriad Greek dishes. Made primarily with sheep's milk and sometimes an addition of up to 30 per cent goat's milk, feta ranges from the very soft, creamy and buttery, to hard, spicy and salty; the more it ages, the harder and spicier it gets.
[2] A dry, anise-flavoured liquor which is served as an aperitif or accompanies food. It is made with a grape or grain distillate in traditional copper cauldrons, flavoured with a variety of herbs, seeds and spices. Uniquely Greek (it can only be made in Greece and Cyprus), it is commonly served diluted in iced water.

Butternut squash fritters with olives and herbs

Fritters made from seasonal vegetables or pulses are prepared in most parts of Greece, using courgettes (zucchini), aubergines (eggplant), potatoes, leeks or mixed leafy greens like spinach and sorrel – even nettles. The islands are particularly big on these kinds of fritters, or *pseftokeftedes* as they call them, meaning 'fake meatballs'. They are primarily a result of the 'poor kitchen' and of the long fasting periods of the past, when methods were invented to replace meat or other animal products.

The fritters are typically fried in order to acquire a crispy outer layer, and although some home cooks now prefer to bake them, I do insist on the traditional fried version – they are delightfully crispy on the outside, moist and fresh on the inside, and they don't feel heavy or oily at all.

The secret for success here is to let the grated butternut drain well and to use plenty of chopped fresh herbs and onions. The fritters are typically served with yogurt or a yogurt-based dip such as *tzatziki*. Here, I pair it with a simple and versatile minty yogurt dip, which you can use in many other recipes.

SERVES 4

350g (12oz) butternut squash, grated (using the big holes of a box grater)
1 tsp salt
1 medium white onion, finely chopped
2 spring onions (scallions), finely chopped
75g (2½oz) pitted green olives, roughly chopped
4 tbsp chopped mint
2 tbsp chopped parsley
2 tbsp chopped dill
2 eggs, lightly beaten
100g (3½oz) feta, crumbled
50g (2oz) plain (all-purpose) flour
1 tsp baking powder
Oil, for frying (I use a light olive oil or sunflower oil)

FOR THE YOGURT DIPPING SAUCE

4 tbsp Greek-style (strained) yogurt
½ tbsp chopped mint
½ tsp ground coriander
½ tsp finely grated lemon zest
2 tsp olive oil
Sea salt and freshly ground black pepper

First prepare the dipping sauce in order for it to be chilled by the time the fritters are ready. In a bowl, combine all the ingredients, adding salt and pepper to taste. Cover and place in the refrigerator.

Place the grated squash in a colander. Add the salt, toss, and let stand for 30 minutes to drain, then squeeze and press it with your hands to remove any last bit of water. Place in a large bowl with the onion, spring onions (scallions), olives, herbs, beaten eggs and crumbled feta. Taste, to check the seasoning, and gently mix until just combined.

Sift the flour and baking powder into the bowl gradually, while mixing. The batter should be a little runny and not too thick or the fritters will be too starchy. Cover with clingfilm (plastic wrap) and place in the refrigerator for 30–60 minutes. (You can skip this step if you are short of time, but it really helps bring out all the flavours in a very nice way and makes it much easier to form the patties.)

Form the patties into ping pong-sized balls and slightly flatten with your hand. Set aside.

Place a deep frying pan over a medium-high heat. Pour oil into the pan to a depth of 1cm (½ inch) and heat. Once hot, add the fritters a few at a time (to keep the oil heat high so that they turn nice and crispy). Fry for about 2–3 minutes on each side or until crispy and golden. Once cooked, place on kitchen paper to soak up excess oil.

Serve with the yogurt dip on the side.

Sautéed olives with onions

This is considered a poor man's dish and was often prepared in times of war and occupation, when food, especially protein, was not abundant. It is based on two staple products all Greeks have always had access to: olives and onions. Olives are treated here as the main ingredient, adding flavour and texture to the softened onions. It is usually made with black olives but I love adding just a few green ones as well. I recommend a type of olive here that is large and meaty – I usually go for a Greek variety called Amfissis (named after Amfissa, a town near Delfi).

Humble dishes such as this are among my favourites: simple, very creative and tasty beyond expectation. You can serve these olives as a sharing plate paired with red wine, but I particularly love serving this as a main dish, with a side of fried potatoes gently soaked in the delightful sauce. You can also serve it sprinkled with crumbled feta, which tastes divine with both the cooked olives and the fried potatoes.

SERVES 4

5 large white onions, halved and fairly
  thickly sliced (5mm/¼ inch slices)
1 tbsp fine sea salt
200g (7oz) pitted black olives
50g (2oz) pitted green olives
150ml (5fl oz) olive oil
2 bay leaves
3–4 allspice berries
¾ tsp sweet paprika
1 tbsp tomato purée (paste)
250ml (9fl oz) red wine
2 tsp dried oregano
4 tbsp chopped parsley
Sea salt and freshly ground black pepper

Mix the sliced onions well with the salt, place in a colander and set aside for about 15 minutes.

Meanwhile, rinse the olives under cold running water, place in a bowl of cold water and leave to soak for 10–15 minutes to desalt them a little, then drain.

Place a large, deep frying pan over a medium heat. Pour in 100ml (3½fl oz) of the olive oil. When the oil is hot, add the onions, bay leaves and allspice. Fry for about 6–7 minutes, stirring occasionally, until the onions soften. Add the sweet paprika and the tomato purée (paste) and stir to combine. Add the olives, gently stir, then pour in the wine. Bring the heat down to low and season with salt and pepper. Gently simmer for 7–10 minutes until most of the liquid is absorbed. Stir in the dried oregano and add the remaining olive oil and chopped parsley. Adjust the seasoning if necessary and gently simmer for another 4–5 minutes until the sauce thickens. Serve plain or with fried potatoes.

Kokoras bardouniotikos, slow-cooked cockerel with feta and green olives

Bardounochoria is a group of villages in the northeast side of the remote and stunning region of Mani, on the south side of the Peloponnese peninsula. Thanks to its rugged and inaccessible landscape, Mani has retained its independent and unique character throughout history. The picturesque and wild Mycenaean ruins, Frankish and Byzantine castles scattered on olive-tree-covered hills, and the rocky coastline create an enchanting scenery that has attracted and inspired writers like Jules Verne, Nikos Kazantzakis and Patrick Leigh Fermor.

As one of the most important regions of Greece for the production of both olive oil and table olives, the simple and delicious local cuisine naturally relies on the extensive use of both. After pork, cockerel is the most popular meat – it is far tastier than chicken, though tougher, which means it needs to be gently slow cooked. You can use a chicken instead, in which case the cooking time will be slightly shorter.

The cheese traditionally used here is called *sfela*[1], an ancient, PDO cheese of the Messinia and Mani regions, also known as 'the cheese of fire'. *Sfela* is not easy to find outside of Greece, but it can be replaced by feta or a combination of feta and a hard cheese like a spicy, aged kefalotyri or pecorino. The green olives add a delightful tangy punch, which makes my tastebuds happy!

The cockerel is usually served over thick spaghetti, bucatini-style pasta or *hylopites*, the traditional Greek egg and milk noodles that either look similar to tagliatelle or can be small and square-shaped – popular with children. It is the perfect dish to prepare for a Sunday family feast.

---

[1] A hard, salty cheese with PDO status, made with sheep's and goat's milk, resembling pecorino and used in a similar way, particularly grated.

SERVES 6

1 cockerel (or free-range chicken), about
  2.5kg (5½lb), cut into portions
100ml (3½fl oz) olive oil, plus a splash for
  the pasta
4 large white onions, roughly chopped
3–4 garlic cloves, finely chopped
2 bay leaves
4–5 allspice berries
1 cinnamon stick
¼ tsp ground cloves
1–2 sprigs of rosemary (or 1 tbsp dried
  rosemary)
4 tbsp red wine vinegar
1 tbsp tomato purée (paste)
500g (1lb 2oz) tomatoes, puréed
  in a blender (or use canned)
150ml (5fl oz) hot water
250g (9oz) feta, crumbled
200g (7oz) pitted green olives
1–2 tbsp chopped parsley
500g (1lb 2oz) thick spaghetti (I like to use
  number 6) or bucatini
Sea salt and freshly ground black pepper

Wash and pat dry the cockerel. Season
with a little salt and pepper and let stand at
room temperature for about 30 minutes.

Meanwhile, place a large, wide pot over
a medium-high heat. Pour in half the olive
oil. Once hot, add the onions, stir and bring
the heat down to low. Season with salt and
black pepper to taste, cover and gently
cook for about 20 minutes until soft and
glossy. Check the onions occasionally while
they are cooking and gently stir to prevent
them from sticking. Once ready, remove
the pot from the heat and, using a slotted
spoon, remove the onions to a plate, leaving
the remaining olive oil in the pot.

Place the pot back over a medium-high
heat. Pour in enough of the remaining olive
oil to just cover the bottom of the pot and,
in batches, brown the cockerel pieces for
about 3–4 minutes on each side, adding
more oil when necessary. Transfer the
browned cockerel to a plate.

Bring the heat down to medium-low, add
the remaining olive oil and gently sauté
together the garlic, bay leaves, allspice,
cinnamon, cloves and rosemary. Add the
vinegar, stir, mix in the tomato purée
(paste) and pour in the tomatoes. Season
with salt and pepper to taste and place the
cockerel pieces back in the pot. When the
sauce is gently simmering, pour in the hot
water. Cover and gently simmer for about
1½ hours until the meat is tender and
falling off the bone, checking occasionally
to make sure it has enough liquid to cook
without burning at the bottom, and adding
a little extra water if needed.

Using a slotted spoon, remove the
cockerel portions from the sauce and place
on a platter. Return the sauce to a medium
heat and add the cooked onions. Gently
stir and simmer, uncovered, for another
15 minutes. Add the crumbled feta and
olives, season with salt and pepper to taste
and let simmer for another 10 minutes until
the sauce thickens. Mix in the chopped
parsley and place the cockerel pieces
back in the sauce.

Meanwhile, cook the pasta in boiling salted
water, according to the packet instructions.
Drain and add a splash of olive oil.

Serve the cockerel over the cooked pasta,
with freshly ground black pepper, and enjoy!

Watermelon summer salad with purslane, capers and feta

The combination of watermelon and feta is an old-school Greek classic that has made a grand comeback. Watermelon works so well with white cheeses and it is a wonderful addition in refreshing summer salads, successfully substituting tomatoes. Ancient Greek doctors used them for hydration, as a diuretic, and to treat sunburn and sunstroke.

Purslane is a weed that grows like crazy during summer – even in random pots on my balcony in downtown Athens. It's packed with vitamins and we use it a lot in salads – even in a regular Greek salad – and other recipes such as stews.

The caper plant is another precious weed widely used in the Greek kitchen. During late spring it starts to grow everywhere, even out of walls and pavements in the centre of Athens. The Acropolis hill is covered in capers throughout summer and the islands are full of large wild caper bushes that climb down steep hills and hang off rocks; those growing near the sea are considered the best. Capers are very nutritious, packed with vitamins, minerals and strong antioxidants, and the ancient Greeks believed in the plant's magical as well as medicinal powers.

The actual caper is a bud that blooms into a stunning white-pinkish flower with a violet stamen, although the leaves can also be preserved and used in recipes. Later on in the summer, the plant produces a little, oblong berry which in Greece we call 'caper cucumbers'. These are also preserved in a similar way as the buds, and they are simply amazing. On certain islands, like Chios, pickled caper berries are stuffed with garlic cloves and served as a lovely meze alongside *tsipouro* or ouzo.

Instead of vinegar, I use *agourida*, also known as verjus (see page 188). It has a fresher, milder flavour compared to vinegar and it's less tangy than lemon – ideal in salads, syrups and cocktails.

SERVES 4–6
1 medium red onion, halved and sliced
450g (1lb) peeled watermelon, deseeded and diced
150g (5oz) teardrop or cherry tomatoes, halved
2 Lebanese cucumbers with skin, sliced into rounds
A bunch of purslane, thick stems discarded, separated into small clusters with leaves
1–2 sprigs of oregano or 1 tsp dried
2 tbsp capers
6–8 Kalamata olives
1 tbsp verjus or red wine vinegar
130g (4½oz) feta, crumbled
100ml (3½fl oz) early harvest olive oil
Flaky sea salt

To soften the sliced onion and make it less astringent, soak in cold water for 10–15 minutes, then drain and pat dry.

Place the watermelon, tomatoes, cucumbers, purslane and onion in a large bowl. Strip the oregano leaves from the stem, if using fresh, and add to the bowl. Add the capers and olives, sprinkle with a little flaky sea salt, and pour in the verjus or vinegar. Gently toss.

Transfer to a salad bowl or platter. Sprinkle with the feta and drizzle with the olive oil.

TIP To deseed a watermelon without ruining its shape, use a toothpick.

Ladenia, baked flatbread with tomato, onions and capers

This recipe originates from Kimolos, a small Cycladic island that sits next to Milos. Legend has it that the island was named after its first inhabitant, who was married to Taurus' daughter, Side. The island has its own popular dishes, but the most famous of all is this pie. Resembling a relatively thick-crusted pizza, this recipe presents *ladenia* in its most basic form, which I adore. It can be 'dressed up' once baked, with some crumbled or flaked cheese (such as feta, aged Greek *graviera*[1], pecorino or Parmesan). For special occasions, or when I wish to pair it with a wine or beer, I like to add thin slices of a cured meat like *louza*[2], sliced prosciutto, or a spicy chorizo.

You will need a large, round and slightly deep baking tin/pan (I use one that is 30–35cm/12–14 inches in diameter).

SERVES 4

FOR THE BASE
500g (1lb 2oz) good-quality plain
  (all-purpose) flour
8g (⅓oz) dried active yeast
1 tsp salt
1 tsp sugar
2 tbsp olive oil, plus extra for oiling
350ml (12fl oz) lukewarm water

FOR THE TOPPING
2 tomatoes, halved and thinly sliced
2 red onions, halved and very thinly sliced
2 tsp dried oregano (wild oregano where
  possible)
70ml (2½fl oz) olive oil
2 tbsp capers (rinsed if salt-packed) or
  sliced Kalamata olives
1–2 tsp oregano leaves
Sea salt and freshly ground black pepper

Sift the flour into a large bowl. Mix in the yeast, salt and sugar, and form a well in the centre.

Pour in the olive oil and water, mix and knead until all the liquid is incorporated. This is a sticky dough that may look a bit lumpy. Don't over-knead, or it will make the final result denser.

Shape your dough into a ball. Generously oil the bowl and dough ball with olive oil, return the dough to the bowl and cover with a dish towel. Leave to rise for about 1 hour 30 minutes until doubled in size.

Preheat the oven to 190°C/170°C fan/ 375°F/gas mark 5. Oil a round 30–35cm/ 12–14 inch baking tin (pan) generously.

Transfer the dough to the tin, without knocking out the air, and spread it out to the edges, using your fingers. Spread the sliced tomatoes and onions on top. Sprinkle with the dried oregano, and some salt and black pepper. Drizzle over the olive oil (be generous, this is called *ladenia – ladi* meaning oil – so the olive oil is key!) and bake on the middle shelf of the oven for 40–45 minutes until golden and crispy and the tomatoes and onions are nicely charred.

Remove from the oven and sprinkle over the capers or olives, fresh oregano and any extra toppings of your choice.

[1] Most commonly prepared with a combination of sheep's and goat's milk, *graviera* can be young or aged and often herbs or spices are added. It can be sliced and eaten, fried, grilled (broiled) or grated.
[2] Greek-style cured pork tenderloin with wine, herbs and spices.

Kakavia, fishermen's soup

This fish soup is among my favourite dishes and one of the most ancient Greek recipes that survives and thrives! It is named after *kakkavion*, an ancient metal cooking pot which was mostly used for boiling and making soups like this one. Invented by Ionian fishermen, the dish is probably the forerunner of French bouillabaisse, from Marseille.

The idea of *kakkavia* was to use the small fish or bony rock fish and other randomly caught seafood the fishermen wouldn't be able to sell. Due to the fact that it was usually prepared on board or on a shore, it is quite simple to make. It is important to use a variety of seafood. The recipe calls for bony rock fish native to the Mediterranean, such as scorpionfish, sea robin, weever, John Dory, comber and wrasse, which give a perfect broth. Small crustaceans, even lobster, are a must to enrich the soup's flavours, and often fishermen will throw in any other random daily catch like mussels or octopus. Small and very bony seafood are usually tied together in a cheesecloth or muslin bag, and if the fish is too small to use for its meat, simply squeeze the bag to retrieve as much flavour as possible, then serve it as a broth with the vegetables.

Potatoes and onions are always included, and olive oil is important (and plentiful) as it thickens and flavours the soup; it is added either at the beginning, before the water (as the fishermen tend to do) or towards the end. I go with the latter so as not to overcook the olive oil and to keep its flavour pleasantly present. Fishermen typically use seawater so salt is not required; at home I use fresh water but always make sure I use high-quality, natural sea salt flakes.

If you can't get a variety of small fish, or if you want meaty fish, feel free to choose a mix of fish commonly found on a fish counter, like hake and monkfish.

SERVES 6

1.2kg (2lb 10oz) mixed fresh fish
  (see introduction)
500g (1lb 2oz) crustaceans (prawns/
  shrimp, crabs, langoustines, lobster,
  crayfish etc.)
5–6 black peppercorns
3 onions
3 potatoes, quartered
4 carrots, sliced into rounds 2cm
  (¾ inch) thick
1 tomato, peeled and halved
4–5 sprigs of celery fronds
3 bay leaves
Pinch of saffron threads
1 small chilli pepper (optional)
170ml (6fl oz) extra virgin olive oil
Juice of 1–1½ lemons, plus extra to serve
Flaky sea salt and freshly ground black
  pepper

Tie all the small fish and other seafood with the peppercorns in a cheesecloth and set aside in the refrigerator until ready to use.

Place the larger fish, if using, in a large pot and add enough water to just cover the fish. Add a pinch of salt and boil for about 20 minutes (depending on size) until done, using a slotted spoon to discard any froth that forms on the surface. Remove the fish from the pot and set aside to slightly cool before you remove the meat from the bones or shells. Strain the fish broth through a fine sieve, in case there are any small bones, and reserve.

Cut a cross halfway down into the onions and place them in the pot along with the rest of the vegetables, bay leaves, saffron and chilli, if using. Place the tied cheesecloth bundle on top. If you poached larger fish, add enough water to top up the poaching broth to 2 litres (70fl oz). If you didn't, then add 2 litres water. Place over

a medium-high heat and bring to the boil, uncovered. (This is a rule when boiling fish, otherwise the smell will be overly fishy.) Simmer gently for about 25 minutes, then remove the cheesecloth bundle, place it in a sieve on top of the pot and press it down to extract the juices.

Add the olive oil and lemon juice to the soup, adjust the seasoning and gently simmer over a low heat for another

5–7 minutes until it thickens. Strain the broth from the vegetables. You can either pulse the vegetables in a food processor and return them to the soup for a thicker result, or serve them alongside the fish to add to your soup once you are ready to serve. Serve warm with extra lemon and black pepper to taste.

Salt cod *brandada* from Santorini

Salt cod, also known as *bacalao*, or in Greek *bakaliaros*, is traditionally prepared with salt-cured Atlantic cod, but nowadays you can find salted fillets of similar fish, like haddock and blue whiting.

Its curing process first began around the late 8th or early 9th century, when the Vikings had the right boats to travel further and needed to have some kind of preservable food on board. Around the early 11th century, cod was introduced to the Basques, who then in turn introduced it to other seamen from Britain and southern Europe. Sailors then adopted the habit of eating cod on board and popularized it in their countries, as it was easy to preserve, very affordable, and simple and versatile to use.

In Greece, salt cod evolved into a staple ingredient, and is included in our National Independence Day dish, celebrated on 25 March. Around the country fried salt cod is served with *skordalia*, an olive-oil-based garlic dip. *Brandada* originally comes from *brandade*, a traditional dish from southern France. The classic French take involves salt cod puréed with milk and garlic, and usually potato, served on sliced bread. The take on the Cycladic Islands is quite different. The cod is cut into portions and is first fried, then the garlicky mashed potatoes are mixed in a simple tomato sauce. The thick sauce is poured over the fried fish, then baked in the oven.

SERVES 4–6
500g (1lb 2oz) potatoes (ideal for
  mashing), peeled and cut into chunks
2 bay leaves
4 garlic cloves, halved
50ml (2fl oz) red wine vinegar
120ml (4fl oz) olive oil
130g (4½oz) plain (all-purpose) flour
½ tsp sweet paprika
750g (1lb 10½oz) salt cod fillet, desalted
  (see page 44) and cut into portions
250ml (9fl oz) light olive or sunflower oil,
  for frying
100g (3½oz) tomato purée (paste)
  (preferably double concentrate)
1½ tsp dried thymbra or thyme
Pinch of sugar
Sea salt and freshly ground black pepper

TO SERVE
1–2 tbsp capers (rinsed if salt-packed)
  or chopped parsley
Drizzle of early harvest
  or extra virgin olive oil

continued…

43

Fill a medium pot with water, add the potatoes, one of the bay leaves, the garlic and a pinch of salt, and boil for about 20 minutes until the potatoes are soft. Drain, reserving some cooking water (about 3 tablespoons), discard the bay leaf and place the potatoes and garlic in a bowl. Mash them well using a potato masher, adding a little of the reserved cooking water if too dry to mash. When nice and smooth, mix in the vinegar, then gradually add the olive oil while working it with the potato masher. Season with salt and pepper to taste and set aside.

Place the flour, a pinch of salt, ½ teaspoon of black pepper and the paprika on a large plate or tray and mix. Dredge the cod fillets, one at a time, in the flour mix, making sure they are coated on all sides, then gently shake off any excess flour.

Place a large frying pan over a medium-high heat. Pour in the light oil for frying, and give it a minute to heat up. Fry the fish, in batches of 2–3 pieces, for 6–7 minutes on each side until golden and crisp. Remove and drain on kitchen paper while you prepare the sauce.

Preheat the oven to 220°C/200°C fan/425°F/gas mark 7.

Place a saucepan over medium-low heat. Before the pan heats up, add the tomato purée (paste) and gradually start pouring in 230ml (7¾fl oz) water while stirring with a whisk until all of it is incorporated. Add the remaining bay leaf and the thymbra or thyme, the sugar, and a pinch each of salt and pepper (take care with the salt), and bring to the boil. Lower the heat, remove the bay leaf, and start mixing in the mashed potato, 1 tablespoon at a time. When all of the potato is incorporated, it should look smooth and relatively thick, and the whole process should not take longer than 5–7 minutes. Remove from the heat (to prevent it thickening further), taste and adjust the seasoning if necessary.

Spoon 2–3 tablespoons of the thick tomato and potato mixture over the base of a deep baking dish, measuring about 20 x 28cm (8 x 11 inches). Place the fried cod on top. Spoon over the tomato and potato mix. Smooth it out with the back of a spoon, then use the back of a fork to create a cross-hatch pattern. Bake in the oven for 25–30 minutes until lightly browned on top, then serve immediately, sprinkled with capers or chopped parsley and drizzled with good-quality olive oil. I like to serve boiled greens, simply dressed with olive oil and lemon juice, on the side.

Desalting cod

The most important step of any recipe involving salt cod is to properly desalt it. You first need to wash it thoroughly under running water. If the fillet is whole, slice it into portions. A fillet weighing about 800g (1¾lb) is usually cut into four or six fairly equal portions. Place the cod in a large glass container (glass is important as it is salt resistant) filled with fresh, cold water and leave to soak. Most recipes call for 24 hours of soaking, but in my opinion it's not enough and I soak it for between 35 and 48 hours, depending on thickness. However, excess soaking can ruin the texture of the flesh, so you need to keep an eye on it. It is important to change the water every 3–4 hours at first, then a little less often. Cover the container each time and place in the refrigerator. When the fish is ready, it will look like a fresh fish fillet again. Strain the water and remove the skin if you like – I usually do, although it is not essential for this particular recipe. If you keep it with the skin, make sure the skin-side faces the bottom of your chosen dish.

Moussaka

There have long been disputes over the origins of moussaka. Whether the recipe comes from Byzantine Greeks, Ottomans, Persians, Palestinians or Arabs, its name has undisputedly Arab roots, deriving from the word *musaqqa'a*, which literally means 'that which soaks up liquid'. Many food historians argue that the recipe was initially inspired by the Persian *maguma*, a dish with lamb and aubergines (eggplants), others claim it has evolved from the Palestinian/Arab *musakhan* (also known as *muhammar*), a dish made with chicken baked with onions and pine nuts and served over a flatbread. Either way, the dish spread to the Middle East, Greece and the rest of the Balkan countries through the Ottomans. The variant that we actually consider as a classic Greek moussaka was re-created in the 1920s by Nikolaos Tselementes (see page 11), who topped it with the bechamel sauce that came to replace the more traditional *yiaourtokoma*, a creamy topping made with yogurt and eggs.

Greek moussaka is always layered and baked in the oven (pictured overleaf). Most Greek cooks (including myself) use sliced potatoes on the base, which are first pan fried. This keeps the shape better as it creates a more stable base, plus the combination works well. The meat most commonly used is minced (ground) beef, or mixed beef and pork, but it can also be made with lamb, and the cheese we tend to use is *kefalotyri* – a hard, salty, goat's and sheep's milk cheese similar to pecorino.

To make the dish lighter, skip the frying bit and instead roast the vegetables as described here.

SERVES 8–10

FOR THE MEAT SAUCE
2 tbsp olive oil
650g (1lb 7oz) minced (ground) beef
  (chuck and blade/shoulder if possible)
1 large onion, chopped
2 garlic cloves, chopped
2 bay leaves
1 cinnamon stick
170ml (6fl oz) dry red wine
600g (1lb 5oz) tomatoes, peeled and
  puréed in a blender, or canned chopped
  tomatoes (with the juices)
1 tsp tomato purée (paste)
½ tsp dried oregano
1½ tbsp chopped parsley
Pinch of sugar (only if the fresh tomatoes
  are not sweet enough)
Sea salt and freshly ground black pepper

FOR THE VEGETABLES
2–3 medium aubergines (eggplants), cut
  lengthwise into 1cm (½ inch) slices
Light olive oil, for frying
3 potatoes, peeled and cut lengthwise into
  1cm (½ inch) slices
3 large courgettes (zucchini), cut
  lengthwise into 1cm (½ inch) slices

FOR THE BECHAMEL
1.5 litres (56fl oz) whole milk
150g (5oz) butter
150g (5oz) plain (all-purpose) flour
Pinch of freshly grated nutmeg
200g (7oz) *kefalotyri* or pecorino cheese,
  grated

continued…

Heat 2 tablespoons of olive oil in a large, wide frying pan. Brown the minced (ground) beef, breaking it up as you stir, for about 5–7 minutes. Add the onion, garlic, bay leaves and cinnamon stick and season with salt and pepper. Stir for a couple of minutes until it looks mostly dry, then pour in the wine and stir again. Add the tomatoes and tomato purée (paste) and turn the heat down to low. If it doesn't look juicy enough, add a bit of water to the mixture. Let it gently simmer, stirring occasionally until most of the liquid is absorbed, 30–40 minutes. Add the oregano and parsley, adjust the seasoning, adding sugar to taste if needed, and give it another stir. Remove the cinnamon stick and bay leaves and set aside off the heat.

batches) turning them until softened and golden on both sides (they don't need to be completely cooked as they will cook further in the oven). Place them on a tray lined with kitchen paper to absorb the excess oil. Season with salt and pepper on both sides.

Heat the milk for the bechamel in a saucepan. Place another large saucepan over a medium heat and gently melt the butter. Add the flour to the butter and mix constantly with a whisk to form a pale roux. Gradually add the warm milk while whisking constantly until you have used all the milk and the sauce thickens (you want it to be medium-thick, not too runny and definitely not too stiff). Stir in the nutmeg and remove from the heat. Season with salt and pepper to taste.

Spoon 5–6 tablespoons of the bechamel sauce into the meat sauce and mix; this makes the meat sauce rich and moist. Mix 3 tablespoons of the grated cheese into the rest of the bechamel.

Preheat the oven to 200°C/180°C fan/400°F/gas mark 6.

In a large, deep baking dish – I use an oval-shaped dish (approximately 30 x 35cm/12 x 14 inches and 7cm/2¾ inches deep) – start layering the potatoes. On top, layer the courgettes (zucchini) and sprinkle with 2 tablespoons of grated cheese. Pour the meat sauce on top and spread out evenly using the back of a spoon. Layer the aubergines on top, pour over some bechamel and sprinkle with a little grated cheese again. Pour over the remaining bechamel and spread it out evenly. Sprinkle with the remaining cheese and bake on a low oven shelf for 40–50 minutes or until golden on top. Remove from the oven and let it cool and settle for at least 20–30 minutes before serving.

In the meantime, start preparing the vegetables. The trick to reduce the bitterness of aubergines (eggplants), and avoid them absorbing more oil, is simply to soak the slices for 15–30 minutes in lukewarm salted water, then pat them dry.

Place a large frying pan over a medium-high heat. Pour in enough oil to cover the base, then pan-fry all the vegetables (in

Peas and leeks braised in olive oil

There is a whole category of recipes in Greek cuisine called *ladera*, meaning 'in oil' or 'oily'. These are seasonal vegetable dishes that are mostly stewed, in either a tomato or lemon sauce, and with a generous amount of olive oil that is added towards the end of cooking to thicken the sauce and add flavour. Many of these recipes evolved from the Byzantine era and the Christian Orthodox tradition, when the Lents and the weekly fasting were entrenched.

This style of cooking greatly defines the essence of the Mediterranean and Greek diet. Recipes of such kind are very popular and are commonly prepared in the average Greek household on a weekly basis, typically using green beans, broad (fava) beans, artichokes, peas, aubergine (eggplant), courgettes (zucchini), okra, leeks and cauliflower. The quality of the olive oil and its flavour will naturally affect the result, and for this I use Koroneiki extra virgin olive oil from the Peloponnese.

Stewed peas are among the most popular *ladera* dishes; they complement the simplicity of flavours in this dish and glorify the presence of olive oil in cooking. I add leeks here for their wonderful yet subtle sweetness. It is due to these delicious and simple vegetable dishes that we Greeks consume so much feta and bread ... do serve these alongside to wipe your dish with!

SERVES 4–6

80ml (2¾fl oz) olive oil, plus 120ml (4fl oz) to finish
2 large onions, chopped
4 leeks, trimmed and cut into rounds 3cm (1¼ inch) thick
2 bay leaves
3 garlic cloves, chopped
3 carrots, cut into 2cm (¾ inch) batons, or sliced
2 potatoes, halved lengthwise then each half quartered
1kg (2lb 3oz) peas, fresh or frozen
¼ tsp ground cinnamon
Pinch of ground allspice
80g (3oz) tomato purée (paste), diluted in 150ml (5fl oz) water
300ml (10fl oz) warm vegetable stock or water
4–5 tbsp chopped dill
Sea salt and freshly ground black pepper

It is best to use a large, wide and fairly shallow pan with a well-fitting lid so the vegetables will cook without losing their shape or going too mushy.

Place your pan over a medium-high heat and pour in the 80ml (2¾fl oz) olive oil. Add the onions and sauté for about 6 minutes until soft and glossy. Add the leeks and bay leaves, and gently cook with the onions until the leeks slightly soften. Add the garlic, carrots, potatoes and peas. Season with salt and black pepper, and add the cinnamon and allspice. Gently stir and pour in the diluted tomato purée (paste), followed by the warm stock or water. Bring the heat down to medium-low, cover and simmer for 30 minutes, then remove the lid and continue to simmer for another 15 minutes, until the sauce is thickened. Pour in the 120ml (4fl oz) olive oil and add the dill. Adjust the seasoning if necessary, gently shake the pot without stirring, and simmer over a low heat for another 5 minutes. Remove from the heat and let it rest for 10–15 minutes before serving.

Mashed potatoes with olive oil, roast garlic and herbs

Potatoes reached Europe during the 16th century, alongside other goods imported from the New World. Potatoes, however, didn't reach Greece until after the Greek War of Independence in 1821 and the emergence of the Modern Greek state in 1830. In fact, it was Ioannis Kapodistrias, the first governor of the newly founded state, who initiated the import of potatoes into the country. He believed that this filling and nutritious tuber would be an ideal food for poor, post-war Greeks. The Greeks, however, didn't trust the new ingredient and when he tried to offer potatoes to farmers in Nafplion, they threw them away! To make them change their minds, Kapodistrias followed the example of Antoine-Augustin Parmentier, the Frenchman who made the French love potatoes. Kapodistrias decided to stop offering them for free. Instead, he started treating them as a superior ingredient. He stored them, fenced them, and he installed guards who pretended to keep watch over them. People started sneaking in to steal them, and within a week all the potatoes were gone.

The best kind of Greek potato is the Naxos variety (a PGI – Protected Geographic Indication – product), which itself instigated the development of cow breeding on the island; locals also noticed that with the use of cow manure, the potatoes grew larger and tastier. The Naxos potato variety is nowadays cultivated in other parts of Greece as well and is the kind of potato I usually go for.

For a variation, mix in about half a cup of crumbled feta; in which case, season with salt after the feta has been added.

SERVES 4–6
1 large head of garlic
1kg (2lb 3oz) potatoes (ideal for mashing), peeled and cut into chunks
½ lemon
1 sprig of thyme
130ml (4½fl oz) olive oil
1–2 tbsp chopped thyme, parsley or dill
Sea salt and white pepper

Preheat the oven to 210°C/190°C fan/410°F/gas mark 6½.

Cut the top off the head of garlic, wrap in baking parchment and then in foil. Bake in the oven for 30–40 minutes, until soft. Squeeze out all the creamy roasted garlic cloves into a bowl and set aside.

Meanwhile, place a large saucepan over a medium-high heat. Add the potatoes, lemon half and thyme sprig, cover with cold water, add salt and bring to the boil. Reduce to medium-low and let simmer for about 15–20 minutes until the potatoes are fork-tender. Drain, reserving 200ml (7fl oz) of the cooking water.

Transfer the potatoes to a large bowl and mash thoroughly using a potato masher or a hand-held mixer on a low speed. (Do not use a food processor because the potatoes will turn gummy.) Gradually start adding some of the reserved cooking water, 1 tablespoon at a time. This will help you smooth it further and bring it to the right consistency.

Add the garlic purée and salt and white pepper to taste, and continue to mash. Gradually start adding the olive oil until it is all incorporated. Finally, mix in the chopped herbs, adjust the seasoning if necessary, and serve.

LEAF

Greece is one of the richest countries in the world for natural, aromatic herbs and edible weeds; it is estimated that over 6,600 kinds of natural herbs grow in Greece, 1,600 of which are listed as medicinal aromatic herbs. These include well known herbs such as rosemary and sage, but also very rare varieties that grow just in specific regions of Greece or in a few parts of the world, such as red oregano.

Here are two of my favourite recipes using olive leaves; one a nice, healing herbal tea and the other a jelly (jello), which is light and refreshing and not too sweet (I only use honey and fresh fruit juice to sweeten jellies). Herbs in these recipes add a discreet yet unique aroma and a pleasant flavour. Dried olive leaves can be found in speciality stores, delis and online. To make easy fresh pomegranate juice, squeeze it just like you would an orange in a citrus juicer.

Olive leaf, hibiscus and pomegranate jelly

MAKES 1 LARGE JELLY
OR 8–10 INDIVIDUAL JELLIES
4 tbsp dried olive tree leaves
4 tbsp dried hibiscus
4 tbsp lemon verbena
2–3 pared strips of lemon zest
(using a swivel peeler)
8 cloves
30g (1oz) powdered gelatine
230g (8oz) honey
500ml (17fl oz) cold, strained pomegranate
juice (see introduction)
Seeds from 1 large pomegranate

Bring 1.5 litres (56fl oz) water to the boil in a medium pan, then turn off the heat and add the olive leaves, hibiscus, verbena, lemon zest and cloves. Cover and let stand for a couple of hours until it turns a deep ruby colour. Strain though a very fine sieve or cheesecloth. Pour 200ml (7fl oz) of the strained room-temperature tea into a small jug (pitcher) or bowl. Sprinkle the gelatine on top and give it 5 minutes to soften. Mix and set aside.

Pour 1 litre (34fl oz) of the herbal tea into a saucepan. Place over a medium heat and gently heat. Remove from the heat and mix in the honey and the gelatine mixture until dissolved.

Mix the pomegranate juice with the remaining 300ml (10fl oz) room-temperature tea. Finally, combine the warm tea mix with the pomegranate mixture. Stir well and strain through a fine sieve into a jelly (jello) mould or individual glasses, and place in the refrigerator for 30 minutes. Add half the pomegranate seeds and place back into the refrigerator for a couple of hours until it sets. Sprinkle with the remaining fresh pomegranate seeds just before serving.

Herbal tea blend with olive leaves

MAKES 1 JAR
1 cup of dried olive tree leaves
1 cup of dried rosebuds
½ cup of dried sage leaves
2 tbsp pink peppercorns
Thyme honey or another sweetener of your
    choice (optional)

Place all the ingredients except the sweetener in an airtight container or jar. Gently toss to mix, then seal.

Use ½ tablespoon of the herbal blend for each cup of tea, add boiling water and let the mixture steep for 5–7 minutes, then strain and add honey or another sweetener to taste. Serve warm or chilled.

GRAIN

The Place of Grains in Greek Culture

Grains are the most ancient and highly consumed food on earth, forming the foundation of the Mediterranean diet.

The use of grains in the ancient Greek kitchen was extensive. No matter the time of day, occasion or social status there was a type of bread available; for example wheat bread (*artos*) was consumed mostly by the upper classes or on festive occasions, while the majority of people consumed barley bread (*alfito*) on a daily basis. In addition to several kinds of breads and cakes, ancient Greeks also used grains to make pies and gruels or porridges.

The local bakers of ancient Athens were considered artisans – the most famous one being Thearion, praised by Plato himself in his book *Gorgias*. Breads and cakes were also prepared to honour the gods – they were often elaborate and shaped according to which god they were offered to. For instance, they offered moon- or deer-shaped breads to Artemis, while Hermes was offered breads shaped as his caduceus (his staff which was entwined by the two serpents). When people were too poor to sacrifice an animal to a god, they would instead offer a bread shaped as an animal. Customs like this still survive in Greek tradition, with elaborate or decorated breads prepared on festive occasions, such as the Easter breads from Crete, known as *avgokouloura,* which are shaped as animals, birds, serpents or fish.

Greek folk tradition includes bread for every single celebration and for all the stages in life, from birth to death. Wheat stands as a symbol for the human body, both in the ancient pagan culture and in the Greek Christian religion, where it symbolizes the body of Christ.

Grains are used in beer-making and other alcoholic drinks, particularly distils which are also used as a base for all sorts of liqueurs or ouzo (when grape distils are not used). Beer-making was practised to a lesser degree by ancient Greeks and Romans; references to beer can be found in the work of Herodotus, but beer was never embraced by the ancient Greeks the way wine was. Proper beer production restarted in the 1850s when the newly appointed king, Otto, who was Bavarian, reinforced beer-drinking within the country. Nowadays Greece produces several kinds of beers and microbreweries thrive.

The Many Different Forms of Wheat

In the Greek kitchen, wheat is used in every stage of its process, from the whole berry to the most processed form of flour. Wheat flour, as in most other cuisines, is and has for centuries been one of the most staple and vital ingredients.

The whole **wheat berries** are the edible part of the wheat kernel, comprising the germ, bran and endosperm. All the nutrients here are intact, which means that wheat berries are packed with fibre and protein and important vitamins and minerals that are lost in the most processed wheat by-products. They are used mainly in salads, as well as breakfast porridges, and in symbolic, ancient recipes which serve as a form of gratitude or offering to the land, in order to guarantee a fertile soil and a good harvest. Wheat berries are symbolic of the cycle of life. The whole berries can even be boiled, their starchy cooking water then used to make a pudding, often with the addition of chopped nuts, seeds, dried fruit and fresh pomegranate seeds. This type of pudding is called *varvara* (*barbara*) in Greek and is annually prepared on 4 December to honour Saint Barbara.

Cracked wheat (also known *hondros* in Greek) and **bulgur** are the ground whole wheat berries (in some cases the outer layer is removed). Bulgur is pre-boiled and dried while cracked wheat isn't. It was mostly used in historic Greek cuisine, in many recipes that now feature rice, and is now used in salads, soups and stuffings. It is cooked along with vegetables or meat as a main course, served as a side, or added to pies and meatballs to absorb excess moisture, add volume and give a fluffier or denser result, depending on the recipe.

Trahanas, or *xinohondros* (see also page 61) is a fermented mixture of wheat and yoghurt or fermented milk. This traditional 'pasta' is particularly popular around Greece since it is fast to prepare, nutritious and filling. It is a staple product and ingredient of the rural regional cuisines of Greece and there are variations in the way it is prepared or shaped in the different areas. The typical way of cooking it is in a form of a savoury or sweet porridge. It is also added in traditional pie fillings and meatballs, to absorb moisture. In recent years *trahanas* has had something of a comeback, featuring on several high-end restaurant menus and in contemporary Greek recipes.

Semolina is finely ground wheat berries, usually made of durum wheat, and is one step before flour-making, but semolina may include a small portion of the bran and germ and is available fine or coarse. It has a lower glycaemic index than regular flour and is rich in nutrients. It is a little coarser and more yellow than white flour due to being less processed, and it looks a lot like polenta, which is more or less the same thing but made of corn. Used in Greece since ancient times to prepare bread, among other things, the best-known is *semidalitis artos* (semolina bread). It is also used as a thickening agent, for instance in soups and custards, in traditional pasta-making, and for breads, types of filo (phyllo) for pies or in filo-less pies (to help them set), traditional cookies and in several cakes.

Pasta Greek mythology talks about a special tool that Hephaistos, god of metalworks and fire, invented in order to shape dough as strings. The first references of *laganon* – a type of pastry made with wheat and water, rolled out and cut into pieces – dates from c. 1,000 BCE. The first Greeks who settled in the south of Italy in around the 8th century BCE brought this recipe with them, which was gradually renamed as *laganum*, the predecessor of lasagne. Both Greeks and Romans cooked early forms of pasta which were initially likely grilled (broiled) rather than boiled. During the Byzantine era there are references to pasta served as dessert, sprinkled with cinnamon and drizzled with honey.

Pasta is widely enjoyed in Greece, and there are several types of handmade local pasta produced in the different regions or for special occasions – such as *gonges*, the carnival pasta that looks a bit like gnocchi and is made in the southern Peloponnese and on Euboea island. During the carnival season, the west and south of Greece serve sweet pasta, boiled in milk then sprinkled with sugar and cinnamon. Of course, the Venetian influence in several parts of the country, specifically the south and the islands, has been crucial in preserving and influencing the techniques of local pasta-making in Greece.

Even though **barley** was the most widely used grain in the past, these days it is mostly included in bread mixes, or for traditional rusks. Barley is also used to make drinks including beer. Rusks, or *paximadia* as they are called in Greek, are a common snack made from different grains or seeds. The name is presumed to derive from a 1st-century CE Greek baker, Paxamos. The recipe originates from the ancient Greek kitchen in what used to be called *dipyros artos*, which basically means twice-baked bread. And that's exactly what rusks are: bread that is sliced and baked again in order to dry and thus last longer. Once a peasant food, rusks are such a big part of Greek culture and are present in the pantry of most households. We eat them as a snack with cheese, olive oil or olives, we add them to soups and salads, we top them with creamy dips and serve them as finger food, and they generally replace bread when it is not available. Rusks enter our lives early as they are often used as a soother for teething babies.

The Arrival of Rice

Rice first arrived in Greece in the 4th century BCE, as a result of Alexander the Great's campaigns in India. Despite its early entry, rice was long regarded as a form of medicine, mostly to cure an upset stomach – as it is still often used. Its culinary use was not really common in Greece before the 1950s and it is due to the Marshall Plan[1] that rice cultivation was encouraged and so became more widespread and cost efficient.

Over time, rice in Greece came to symbolize abundance and prosperity. It's not uncommon to find *gamopilafo* – a rustic risotto-style dish from the island of Crete cooked in goat broth – commonly served at traditional weddings and other large festivities. At Christmas and New Year, chickens and turkeys are stuffed with rice, while at Easter, lamb is often stuffed with rice for similar symbolic reasons.

Nowadays, rice is a staple ingredient in Greek cuisine; to a large extent, it has replaced the use of cracked wheat and has become a key ingredient in many savoury as well as sweet recipes.

The five main types of rice used in traditional Greek recipes are: Carolina, Nyhaki, Glacé, Yellow and Bonnet (par-boiled).

[1] A USA aid programme aimed at supporting and developing European economies in the wake of the Second World War. One of its initiatives in Greece was to train farmers on rice growing and production. Now the country grows enough rice to meet domestic demand and export as well.

Welcoming Corn

Corn reached Europe after the discovery of America, along with other products such as tomatoes, beans and peppers. Arriving in Greece around 1600 (which at the time was mostly Ottoman occupied) via North Africa, the Greeks named it *aravositos*, which means 'wheat of the Arabs'. Its use became associated with poverty and war, as it replaced other staple grains that were harder to get hold of during periods of economic hardship. This is evident in the modern-day use of cornmeal in pies and other recipes such as *tzaletia* from Corfu (pancakes, see page 133). Cornflour (cornstarch) is also widely used to thicken soups and sauces and in pastry creams and custards. The Ionian islands mostly adopted the use of polenta, mainly due to the Venetian influence on the local cultures.

It is a typical summer tradition all around Greece to find street vendors grilling corn on the cob and serving it with butter and sea salt. This and an ice-cold beer is one of my favourite snacks while enjoying a movie at open-air summer cinemas around Greece!

Mighty Pies

Pies are a massive chapter of Greek cuisine; their history stretches back to the ancient Greeks and they probably deserve a whole book to themselves. There are so many kinds and methods, and so many names and fillings. Representing every region's bounty and local produce, pies were a salvation for agricultural families, particularly the women-heroes who did it all: worked all day in the fields, took care of their household and large families and cooked for everyone. Nutritious, filling, and above all tasty, the large humble pie has fed generations of Greeks for several centuries.

Greek pies are often enclosed in filo (*phyllo*) pastry, which literally means 'leaf' in Greek. There are several different kinds of filo, prepared with different ingredients and methods, some ultra-thin and multi-layered, some medium or thick and single layered. In addition, several Greek pies are prepared without any filo, or with filo scraps, while others resemble a pizza, like *ladenia* from Kimolos (see page 38).

Trahanas and cherry tomato soup with yogurt, feta and basil

Trahanas (see page 56) is often described as a 'rustic pasta' – a staple, humble ingredient with a pastoral background and origins that can be traced back to ancient times. It is now found in the cuisines of mostly southeastern European countries and the Middle East. The most common types are dairy-based and come in two main categories: sweet and sour.

There are many regional variations of this homely dish. It was commonly prepared in villages in mid- to late-summer, after the wheat harvest – when milk was abundant and there was enough heat and breeze for drying – as a means of preservation for winter. The rustic way of cooking *trahanas* is similar to porridge and it is traditionally served as a winter breakfast in mountain areas or as a comforting meal for either lunch or dinner.

SERVES 4

4 tbsp olive oil
1 small onion, finely chopped
2 garlic cloves, minced
350g (12oz) cherry tomatoes, quartered
1 bay leaf
1 litre (34fl oz) boiling water or vegetable stock
180g (6oz) *trahanas* (ideally sour, but sweet will work)
2 tbsp Greek-style (strained) yogurt
100g (3½oz) feta, crumbled
2–3 tbsp chopped basil
Sea salt and freshly ground black pepper
Extra virgin olive or chilli oil, to serve

Place a heavy-based pan over a medium heat. Once hot, pour in the olive oil and let it heat up a little. Add the onion and garlic and stir for a few minutes until the onion is soft and glossy. Add the tomatoes and bay leaf, season with salt and pepper, and stir for 3–4 minutes. Pour in the boiling water or stock and bring to the boil. Add the *trahanas*, stir and reduce the heat to medium-low. Gently simmer, stirring constantly, for 5–8 minutes until it starts to thicken. The more you cook it, the thicker it will get, so don't overdo it. Remove from the heat and mix in the yogurt, crumbled feta and basil. To serve, drizzle with a bit of extra virgin olive oil or chilli oil, and season with extra pepper if desired.

To reheat from cold (it will have set), add a little boiling water to dilute.

Koftopita, festive cheese and cracked wheat pie with handmade filo

The mountainous region of Epirus, in northwest Greece, is particularly famous for its pies, as well as for its wonderful dairy products, including its PDO feta. Some of the region's many pies are made for special occasions, including this *koftopita* (pictured on page 66), which is rich and filling, with milky and buttery aromas.

This filo (phyllo) recipe is a classic. You can use it in multiple ways, and if you wish to roll out more, thinner filo sheets, you simply divide the dough into more pieces, following the same process as described here. You can also double the recipe for a larger pie, or use the pastry to make small, individual pies.

The traditional way of rolling out thin filo requires a large, round wooden surface known as *plastiri* (shaper). Usually made of oak, it is a great tool for rolling out ultra-thin doughs for pies or pasta. Older women in villages roll out filo on tablecloths, but their expertise goes far beyond special tools and props! What is definitely required for best results, however, is a long, thin rolling pin resembling a broomstick – a *verga*, meaning stick. The whole technique of rolling out Greek filo lies in the way you use this rolling pin, artfully furling and unfurling the dough on it until it's perfectly thin, round and not sticky. It's not as hard as it may sound or look and practice definitely makes perfect. For me this is the ultimate form of meditation – relaxing and joyful.

Filo and Pie Tips

Baking trays (sheets) and tins (pans) made from tin alone are best. They don't need to be very deep.

Use the conventional oven setting to bake the bottom and top evenly.

To achieve a crisp filo, you need to generously brush each layer with olive oil or melted butter (depending on the recipe).

With thin hand-made filo, use two or more layers; with thicker filo, do single layers.

The amount of flour you use in the dough depends on the weather (humidity levels) and the flour. Add the water gradually, while kneading, in order to control it. I leave the last third of water to wet my hands while I knead and when I feel the dough is soft and elastic and not sticky, I stop adding water.

This filo recipe can be used with other pie fillings and all the recipes can be adapted to use store-bought filo.

MAKES 1 PIE

FOR THE FILO (PHYLLO)
350g (12oz) plain (all-purpose) flour, sifted,
  plus extra for rolling
½ tsp fine sea salt
1 tsp white vinegar
3 tbsp olive oil, plus extra for brushing
160–180ml (5½–6fl oz) lukewarm water

FOR THE FILLING
80g (3oz) cracked wheat (coarse)
130ml (4½fl oz) whole milk, plus 100ml
  (3½fl oz)
Pinch of salt
4 eggs, at room temperature
450g (1lb) feta, crumbled
30g (1oz) butter, softened
Freshly ground black pepper, to taste

For the filo

In a large bowl, combine the flour and
salt. Add the vinegar and olive oil and mix
with your hands, rubbing the mix with
your fingertips until the vinegar and oil are
fully absorbed by the flour. Gradually start
pouring in the water, while kneading. Do
it very gradually as you knead, because it
might not need it all (see Tips, opposite).
You can also do this in a stand mixer with
a dough hook.

Knead for 10–15 minutes until nice and
smooth, soft and not sticky. Shape into a
ball and wrap in clingfilm (plastic wrap).
Let rest at room temperature for 1–2 hours.
If you are planning to roll out the dough
later, you can cover with clingfilm, place
in the refrigerator and bring it to room
temperature for about an hour before rolling
it out. You can make the filling while you
wait for the dough to rest (before rolling it
out), see page 67.

To roll out the filo nice and thin, you will
need a long, thin rolling pin for pastry. Clear
a large, clean, ideally wooden work surface
and have ready a baking tin (pan), about
30cm (12 inches) in diameter and 3cm
(1¼ inches) deep. The diameter of the rolled
out filo should be large enough to reach
beyond the edges of the tin once laid in it,
so you will need to use something with a
large enough surface, like a table.

Tip a little flour into a small bowl. Divide
the dough into four and shape each piece
into a ball.

Generously dust the work surface with
flour. Smooth out the dough with your
hands and press each ball down with your
hand to form flat discs. Flip them over on
the flour and stack them one on top of the
other (coating them with flour will prevent
them from sticking to each other). Cover
with a dish towel (if the weather is very dry,
use a damp dish towel).

Dust again with flour. Take the first disc
and place it in the centre of your work
surface. Roll it out gently into a larger circle.
Dust the top of the dough with a little flour,
rubbing it around the surface. You want to
keep the filo dry so that it will furl onto the
pin without sticking at all. Keep dusting
and rolling (furling) it gently onto the rolling
pin all the way. As you roll it on the pin, use
both hands to gently put some pressure
outwards; this will widen the filo. Repeat
the same process from different angles in
order to maintain the round shape, until it is
paper thin. (For best results follow my step-
by-step photos overleaf.) Repeat with the
rest of the dough. I usually transfer directly
to the tin while I assemble the pie, but if
not, place baking parchment between each
filo sheet and always keep covered with
a damp dish towel.

continued…

For the filling

Place the cracked wheat in a fine sieve and rinse under running water, then drain. Pour 100ml (3½fl oz) water into a medium pot, place over a medium heat and bring to the boil. Add the wheat and simmer, uncovered, for about 10 minutes until most of the water is absorbed. Add the 130ml (4½fl oz) milk and salt and continue to simmer for 5–10 minutes, stirring occasionally with a wooden spoon to prevent it from sticking, until the milk is absorbed and the cracked wheat is cooked. Remove from the heat, mix with a spoon and allow it to cool down for 5–10 minutes.

Meanwhile, in a large bowl, whisk the eggs, then mix in the crumbled feta. Once the wheat has slightly cooled, gradually spoon it into the egg mixture with the butter and stir well to incorporate. Mix in the remaining 100ml (3½fl oz) milk, adjust the salt, if necessary, and add black pepper to taste.

To assemble

Preheat the oven to 240°C/220°C fan/475°F/gas mark 8 (use a conventional oven setting, if possible).

Pour some olive oil into a small bowl. Using a brush, generously grease the base and sides of the tin with olive oil. Using the rolling pin to lift the pastry, carefully transfer the first filo sheet into the centre of the greased tin, making sure it properly sits in the base and that the filo reaches beyond the edges of the tin.

Brush with olive oil. Repeat with the second filo sheet, without greasing it with oil. Spoon in the filling, spreading it out evenly with the back of a spoon. Using the same brush, sprinkle a bit of olive oil on the filling and lightly grease the excess filo around the edges. Fold the excess filo over the filling all the way around the tin. Brush these folded-in sides with a bit of olive oil. Place the next filo sheet on top of the filling and brush with a generous amount of olive oil (the top filo sheets need a bit more olive oil in order to be nice and crispy in the end). Repeat with the remaining filo sheet.

Using scissors or a knife, trim the excess filo around the edges, leaving about 2–3cm (¾–1¼ inches). Twist the edges inwards, going all the way around to seal the pie and form a nice rim (for best results follow my step-by-step photos on pages 64–65). Using a sharp knife, score the pie, brush generously with olive oil and sprinkle with a bit of water on top.

Place on a low oven shelf, turn the oven down to 200°C/180°C fan/400°F/gas mark 6 (still on the conventional setting, if possible) and bake for 10–15 minutes, then turn the oven down to 180°C/160°C fan/350°F/gas mark 4 and bake for a further 35–40 minutes, or until golden and crispy on top. For best results, spray it with a bit of water two or three times while it is baking.

Remove from the oven and allow it to cool down for at least 30 minutes before you cut into it.

Barley with smoked trout and pork sausage

The first written references to sausages in Greek cuisine can be traced back to Homer's epics. The ancient Greeks loved sausages and developed various techniques of curing and preserving meats, most of which were passed on to the Romans. Sausages were made with chopped meat and often offal, mixed with herbs and spices, as well as other ingredients such as leek, wheat or other grains, pine nuts, lard or blood. Today, the most prevalent type of sausage is made of pork, spiced in various ways, but other regional variations include beef, buffalo and sheep.

I love combining pork and seafood, especially trout with sausage. I serve this as a warm winter salad or a meze dish that pairs fantastically well with beer or *tsipouro*. This dish can also be prepared with other grains or seeds.

SERVES 4–6

250g (9oz) barley or wheat berries
1 tbsp olive oil
120g (4oz) pork sausage, halved
  lengthwise and sliced
120g (4oz) smoked trout fillets
3 spring onions (scallions), including the
  green part, chopped
3 tbsp chopped dill
2 tbsp chopped parsley

FOR THE DRESSING
1 tbsp orange juice
2 tbsp lemon juice
½ tbsp Dijon mustard
6 tbsp extra virgin olive oil
Finely grated zest of 1 orange
Sea salt and freshly ground black pepper

Boil the barley or wheat according to the packet instructions (for wheat you might need to soak it overnight). Let stand in a colander to drain.

Prepare the dressing. Mix the orange and lemon juices with the mustard until combined. Gradually whisk in the olive oil, then mix in the orange zest and season with salt and pepper.

Heat the olive oil in a deep frying or sauté pan over a medium-high heat and fry the sausage pieces, flipping them over to cook evenly until they brown slightly. Remove from the pan.

Lower the heat to medium-low and add the trout fillets. Gently heat through for about 1 minute on each side then remove from the pan. Add the drained barley or wheat berries to the pan, tossing with a spoon to heat up and evaporate any excess water. Mix in the sausage and keep tossing. Remove from the heat and mix in the dressing while tossing, then finally mix in the spring onions (scallions), dill and parsley. Cut the trout fillets into smaller pieces and place them on top to garnish, or mix them into the wheat.

Artichoke and caper stuffed calamari

This is not a common or traditional recipe from any part of Greece; it is my own invention. I was inspired by the ways calamari is stuffed in Greece, often involving rice or just tomatoes and feta. The artichokes pair really well here with the herbs, as does the calamari with the tangy citrusy sauce. When I have friends over and I wish to turn this dish into something more shareable, I simply slice them like sushi rolls; they are easier to eat that way, and also look beautiful. This is great with a good retsina wine.

SERVES 4-6
6 large calamari, each about 400g (14oz)
3 tbsp olive oil
100ml (3½fl oz) dry white wine
100ml (3½fl oz) warm vegetable stock
  or water

FOR THE FILLING
2 tbsp olive oil
1 large onion, chopped
5 spring onions (scallions), chopped
300g (10½oz) artichoke hearts, fresh or
  frozen, cut into small chunks
100ml (3½fl oz) dry white wine
1½ tbsp lemon juice
150ml (5fl oz) warm vegetable stock
  or water
50g (2oz) cracked wheat
3 tbsp chopped dill
3 tbsp chopped parsley
2 tbsp capers (rinsed if salt-packed),
  roughly chopped
Finely grated zest of 1 small lemon
Sea salt and freshly ground black pepper

FOR THE LEMON AND DILL SAUCE
40ml (1½fl oz) lemon juice
125ml (4fl oz) olive oil
1 tbsp chopped dill

Wash and clean the calamari. Set aside in a colander to drain.

For the filling, place a large pan over a medium heat. Add the olive oil and sauté the onion for 6–7 minutes until soft and glossy. Add the spring onions (scallions) and artichokes, and stir for a couple of minutes until the artichokes soften. Pour in the wine, wait for a minute or so, then add the lemon juice and stock or water and turn the heat down to medium-low. Mix in the cracked wheat, season with salt and pepper and gently simmer for about 10 minutes, until most of the liquid has been absorbed and the artichokes are fork-tender. Remove from the heat and mix in the herbs, capers and lemon zest.

Using a teaspoon, stuff the calamari with the artichoke filling, pushing the filling down into the tubes with the back of the spoon. Seal the tentacle end using two toothpicks for each calamari, attaching the tentacles to the sticks too – make sure you haven't over-stuffed so that they don't seal with the toothpicks. Pierce the body here and there with a toothpick to prevent it from bursting while cooking.

Place a wide pot with a tight-fitting lid over a medium heat and add 2 tablespoons of the olive oil. Once hot, place in the stuffed calamari. They will sizzle. Let them cook for a couple of minutes on each side, flipping them over. Season with salt and pepper, then pour in the wine, followed by the warm stock or water, and drizzle with the remaining tablespoon of olive oil. Season with a little black pepper and cover with the lid. Cook for about 20–30 minutes until most of the liquid has been absorbed and the calamari are fork-tender.

Meanwhile, make the dressing. Add the lemon juice to a bowl. Slowly pour in the olive oil while whisking quickly. It should look rather yellowish and thickened. Mix in the dill along with salt and pepper to taste.

Serve the calamari either whole or sliced, drizzled with the sauce.

Kollyva, wheat berry and nut mixture

The third and final day of one of the most important annual ancient Greek celebrations, *Anthesteria*, was dedicated to the dead. As part of the celebration, *panspermia* (now known as *kollyva*) was prepared to honour Hermes, the god who led the dead to the underworld. *Panspermia* was a mix of nuts and grains that each symbolized a stage in the cycle of life and these days it is offered at funerals.

Aside from its symbolic meaning, this is a treat for breakfast or even as a light dessert. As well as serving it plain, I also love serving it on Greek-style (strained) yogurt, custard, or ice cream, or sprinkled on fruit salads.

SERVES 6-8

180g (6oz) wheat berries
1 bay leaf
50g (2oz) pistachios
50g (2oz) walnuts
50g (2oz) flaked (slivered) almonds, lightly toasted
4 tbsp toasted sesame seeds
3 tbsp fine dried breadcrumbs (ideally from rusks or melba toast), lightly toasted in a pan, plus an extra 1 tbsp if needed
Pinch of salt
50g (2oz) icing (confectioners') sugar
1 tbsp ground cinnamon
½ tsp ground cloves
2 tbsp sunflower seeds
1 tbsp nigella seeds
50g (2oz) currants
50g (2oz) raisins
1 tsp finely grated lemon zest
3-4 tbsp pomegranate seeds
3 tbsp chopped parsley (or coriander/cilantro leaves)

Place the wheat berries in a bowl, cover with water and soak overnight. The following day, rinse and drain.

Place the wheat berries in a medium pan, cover with fresh water, add the bay leaf and place over a medium-high heat. Boil for about 30 minutes or until cooked, then drain and rinse until the water runs clear. Discard the bay leaf and let the wheat berries stand in a colander for about 40 minutes to drain well and cool down. Lay a clean dish towel on a large tray and spread out the cooked and drained wheat berries. Cover with a second clean dish towel and let the wheat berries dry further for another 2–3 hours, rubbing them occasionally with the top towel until fully dried.

Meanwhile, coarsely chop all the nuts. Reserve 1 tablespoon of the sesame seeds to mix in at the end, and grind the rest of the seeds to a powder in a food processor.

In a large bowl, combine the powdered sesame seeds with the dried wheat berries, breadcrumbs, salt and icing (confectioners') sugar. Add the cinnamon and cloves, and mix with a spoon. If the mixture still looks a bit wet, add some extra breadcrumbs (no more than an extra tablespoon). Mix in the chopped nuts, the seeds, currants, raisins, lemon zest, pomegranate seeds and parsley.

Gemista, rice-stuffed vegetables

My most vivid memory of *gemista* ('stuffed') is preparing it as a kid with my grandmother, Rena, at her summer house on the island of Aegina. Down the street from her house was a lovely old bakery with a traditional wood-burning oven. It was common back then for people to prepare food at home in the morning and then take it to their local baker to bake in their oven, which had exceptional results and gave the food nice, smoky flavours.

This popular recipe is prepared all over Greece, in various ways. It usually involves stuffing tomatoes and green peppers with rice and/or minced (ground) meat and baking in the oven with chunks of potato squeezed between the vegetables. The meat-free version – a summer favourite – is known as '*orfana*' (orphans) and is best eaten at room temperature with a large chunk of feta on the side, fresh crusty bread and cold beer. Although most variations are baked, some are prepared in a pot on the stovetop.

Tomatoes are the steadfast star here. You will need plenty of them, not just for stuffing but also for the sauce. The tomatoes you use must be in season, medium-large and ripe enough to scoop them out without tearing the outer layer.

I recommend making a big batch of these as they keep really well in the refrigerator for a couple of days. The recipe is also easy to adjust using alternative grains.

SERVES 8–10

5 medium, juicy, ripe tomatoes, plus an extra one (or canned tomatoes) if needed
2–3 green (bell) peppers
1 red (bell) pepper
1 medium aubergine (eggplant)
2–3 chubby courgettes (zucchini)
5 medium potatoes, peeled, cut in half crosswise and quartered
4–5 tsp fine dried breadcrumbs
Sea salt and freshly ground black pepper

FOR THE STUFFING

300g (10½oz) medium-grain white rice (ideally Carolina)
50ml (2fl oz) olive oil
2 large onions, chopped
2 large garlic cloves, chopped
1 large carrot, grated
1½ tsp dried oregano
2 handfuls of chopped parsley
2 handfuls of chopped mint

FOR THE SAUCE

280g (10oz) ripe tomatoes
150ml (5fl oz) olive oil
1 tsp dried oregano

Preheat the oven to 200°C/180°C fan/400°F/gas mark 6.

Wash the vegetables for stuffing, and pat them dry. Neatly slice off the top part (so it can work as a lid). Start with the tomatoes, scooping out their insides with a teaspoon. Put all the tomato pulp in a blender and briefly pulse. You will need 700ml (24fl oz) pulp. If the tomatoes were not juicy enough to leave you with the required amount of juice, add an extra one or mix in some processed canned tomatoes.

Remove all seeds from the (bell) peppers and discard. Next, scoop out the aubergine (eggplant) and courgettes (zucchini) and finely chop the flesh you have removed. If you find the courgettes tricky, you can halve them lengthwise, hollow them out and then when you stuff them, sandwich them back together.

To make the stuffing, place the rice in a colander and rinse well with cold water.

Place a large, deep pan over a medium-high heat. Add the olive oil and sauté the onions for a couple of minutes until golden. Add the garlic, chopped courgette and aubergine flesh, and the grated carrot.

continued…

Stir for 1 minute, then add the rice, season with salt and pepper to taste and stir for a couple of minutes. Add the tomato pulp and cook for another minute, then pour in 200ml (7fl oz) water. Continue to stir for 10–12 minutes until most of the liquid has been absorbed (it should not look completely dry, but rather still be juicy, almost like a creamy risotto, but the rice must still be undercooked or it will go mushy later). Remove from the heat and stir in the dried oregano and fresh herbs. Add salt and pepper to taste and stir well.

Next, start filling the hollowed-out vegetables with the rice mixture, using a teaspoon. Don't overstuff them, as the rice will expand when properly cooked. Place the tops of the vegetables back on and place them in a large, deep baking dish. If you have leftover stuffing, you may stuff a few extra vine leaves (if using, see opposite) or a pepper. Alternatively, store in the freezer and use it next time.

Mix the potatoes with salt and pepper in a bowl, and wedge them between the vegetables in the baking dish.

Put the tomatoes for the sauce in a blender along with the olive oil and 200ml (7fl oz) water. Pulse until smooth, season with salt and pepper, and mix in the dried oregano. Pour the tomato sauce on top and around the stuffed vegetables, then sprinkle the breadcrumbs over the top. Bake on the lowest oven shelf for about 1½ hours, uncovered, until the tops look slightly charred and caramelized, the vegetables are soft, and most of the liquid in the dish has evaporated, leaving a thickened sauce.

Remove from the oven and let stand for at least 15–20 minutes before serving.

Cretian variation:
Stuffed courgette (zucchini) flowers and vine leaves

3–4 courgette flowers
3–4 vine leaves, blanched (see page 220)

Remove the stamen carefully from the flowers and use a teaspoon to stuff, leaving enough space to fold the top of the flower and seal (you can use toothpicks to seal). For stuffed vine leaves, follow the folding instructions on page 220, blanching them first and adding a couple of teaspoons of filling. Proceed as for the main recipe.

Spanakoryzo, spinach rice

This is a kind of simplified, light risotto, although here the spinach dominates the rice, while the herbs, olive oil and lemon juice all play a big part in the final result. Similar variations are prepared with other vegetables, thus seasonality is vital as the star vegetable will mostly flavour the dish. During summer we make *melitzanoryzo* (aubergine/eggplant rice) or *tomatoryzo* (tomato rice), during winter it's often *prasoryzo* (leek rice) or *lachanoryzo* (cabbage rice). Spring calls for courgette (zucchini) flower rice, while this *spanakoryzo* is prepared year-round, with other greens if spinach is not available.

Spinach in Greece is sold whole, in leafy bunches with the root tips still present, holding the leaves together. Whenever using spinach in a recipe, traditional – mostly rural – cooks would commonly keep the root tips and stalks after removing them, to prepare a second simple dish, such as a boiled salad with lemon and olive oil.

This is among my favourite dishes: humble, comforting, nutritious and full of flavour. The secrets to this recipe's success, apart from using fresh produce, are to avoid adding too much water and to avoid overcooking it, as the rice will become mushy and the spinach will lose its texture and vibrant colour. My tip is to always use fresh spinach and a high-quality extra virgin olive oil, which will greatly impact the final flavour. Always add herbs towards the end to keep their flavours and aromas more intense. The type of rice here is very important too. We traditionally use Carolina[1] in this sort of dish, but Arborio or Bomba can also be used. Serve this with feta and crusty bread.

SERVES 4

250g (9oz) medium-grain white rice
Juice of ½ lemon
120ml (4fl oz) olive oil
1 large onion, chopped
1 leek, trimmed and chopped
5 spring onions (scallions), including the
  green part, chopped
1 small garlic clove, minced
1kg (2lb 3oz) fresh spinach, washed well
  and trimmed (avoid baby spinach here)
600ml (20fl oz) hot water
4–5 tbsp roughly chopped dill
50ml (2fl oz) lemon juice, plus extra if
  wished
Sea salt and freshly ground black pepper

Place the rice in a colander and rinse thoroughly under cold running water. Drain, then mix with juice of half the lemon and allow to drain again (this will keep the texture of the rice firmer).

Place a large, wide, shallow pan over a medium-high heat. Pour in 3 tablespoons of the olive oil and sauté the onion and leek until soft. Add the spring onions (scallions) and garlic and stir for another minute. Add the spinach in batches until wilted. (You can roughly chop the spinach, but I like to keep it as whole as possible so that it doesn't overcook). Season with salt and pepper, sprinkle in the rice, gently stir, then pour in the hot water.

Turn the heat down to medium-low and gently simmer for about 15–20 minutes until the rice is cooked, stirring occasionally. Do not cover as this will make the spinach lose its vibrant green colour. Bring the heat down to low, add the dill, the rest of the olive oil and the lemon juice, and stir. Gently cook for another couple of minutes, stirring now and then. Remove from the heat and allow to sit for at least 10 minutes. Serve seasoned with extra lemon juice, if desired.

[1] Produced in Serres, northern Greece, Carolina rice is white and medium-grain, very absorbent, high in starch and cooks quickly. It is used in traditional braised vegetable and rice dishes, meatballs and soups, in stuffed vegetables and wrapped leaves (*dolmades*).

Chicken soup with *avgolemono*

Every culture around the world has a restorative chicken soup. For Greeks it is *kotosoupa avgolemono*. I cannot think of a more comforting dish than this one. The creaminess here is due to the rice, which should be rich in starch, and the egg and lemon sauce, *avgolemono*, which also gives it a nice velvety texture. It is a soup enjoyed in Greece throughout winter, and my grandmother Rena, who was a master of this soup, always made it on New Year's Day.

It is traditionally served as a thick broth with the rice in it, with the left-over boiled chicken often used for a chicken pie. I like to also add carrot and courgette (zucchini) for flavour and texture, but you can play around with different vegetables. I always buy a high-quality chicken, preferably organic or free-range: they have less fat and are full of flavour.

SERVES 4–6

1 x 1.8–2kg (4–4½lb) chicken, cut into
  6 pieces
1 tbsp olive oil
1 large onion, peeled and halved
1 small leek, roughly chopped
2 garlic cloves, peeled
1 large celery stick, trimmed and roughly
  chopped
2 bay leaves
6 black peppercorns
3–4 sprigs of thyme
1 small tomato
80ml (3fl oz) dry white wine
1.5 litres (56fl oz) hot water
2 large carrots, diced
120g (4oz) medium-grain white rice, such
  as glacé (glutinous)
2 small courgettes (zucchini), diced
2 eggs, at room temperature
Finely grated zest of 1 small lemon and
  juice of 2
Sea salt and freshly ground black pepper
1 tbsp chopped spring onions (scallions),
  including the green part (optional),
  to serve

Wash the chicken well, pat dry and set aside. (Keep the giblets for another time.)

Place a large, heavy pan over a medium-high heat. Add the olive oil and gently sauté the onion, leek, garlic, celery, bay leaves, peppercorns and thyme for about 8 minutes, stirring, until softened. Add the chicken, turning the pieces until slightly browned all over. Add the tomato (whole) and pour in the wine. Season with salt and pour in the water. Cover, reduce the heat to medium-low and simmer for 50–60 minutes until the chicken is thoroughly cooked.

Transfer the chicken to a platter and let it cool. Remove the skin and bones, then shred or cut the meat into small pieces.

Strain the broth and pour it back into the pot. Return it to the stovetop, turn the heat up to medium-high and adjust the salt if necessary. Add the carrots and bring to the boil. When it starts boiling, reduce the heat to medium and add the rice. Let it boil for 10 minutes, then finally add the courgettes. Boil for another 10 minutes until the veggies and rice are cooked.

Remove the pan from the heat. Ladle about 200ml (7fl oz) of broth through a sieve into a jug (pitcher) and set aside. Separate the eggs into two bowls. Beat the yolks with the lemon zest and juice. Whisk the egg whites into a light meringue (not too stiff). Gradually whisk the egg yolks into the whites until incorporated (don't over-whisk).

Carefully and gradually add small amounts of the strained hot soup to the egg and lemon sauce, whisking constantly. The sauce should look nice and frothy. Once the soup is all incorporated, pour the mixture into the pot and stir gently.

Serve the soup with shredded chicken and spring onions (scallions), if desired, and a grind of black pepper.

Yiouvarlakia, hearty meatball soup

This is one of my favourite Greek comfort dishes. It's popular all over the country and is most commonly prepared with egg and lemon sauce, like this one, or – often during summer – in a tomato-based broth. It was a dish prepared by Greeks settled in Asia Minor who popularized it in Greece in the early 1920s, along with several other recipes that greatly shaped what is called the Urban Athenian Cuisine. What makes the Greek version different to others is the use of egg and lemon sauce, and the herbs or spices. In parts of northern Greece and particularly in Naoussa (a famous wine region), this dish is also known as *koukoulia* (which means cocoons).

Yiouvarlakia is usually prepared with plain minced (ground) beef or a combination of half beef, half pork. The sauce here works both as a flavour enhancer and as a thickener for the broth, giving the soup a lovely creamy consistency. Good bread is essential when serving this dish – trust me.

SERVES 4–6

FOR THE MEATBALLS
120g (4oz) medium-grain white rice
750g (1lb 10½oz) minced (ground) beef
1 large onion, finely chopped
1 large carrot, grated
1 egg
2 tbsp chopped mint
2 tbsp chopped dill, plus extra to serve
2 tbsp chopped parsley
100ml (3½fl oz) olive oil
2 tsp fine sea salt
1 tsp freshly ground black pepper

FOR THE BROTH
3 tbsp olive oil
1 leek, chopped
1 celeriac (celery root), peeled and diced
  into 2cm (¾-inch) cubes (prepared
  weight 450g/1lb)
2 potatoes, peeled and cut into 1.5cm
  (½ inch) cubes
3 carrots, cut into 1.5cm (½ inch) cubes
1 bay leaf
2 litres (70fl oz) warm vegetable stock
  or water
Sea salt and freshly ground black pepper

FOR THE AVGOLEMONO
2 eggs, at room temperature
90ml (6 tbsp) lemon juice
1 tbsp cornflour (cornstarch)

To make the meatballs, rinse the rice and soak in cold water for 15–20 minutes. Drain and let dry.

Place the beef in a bowl. Add the onion, carrot, egg, chopped herbs, olive oil, rice, salt and black pepper. Combine well, then cover and place in the refrigerator for at least 15 minutes. (You can fry a small amount of the mixture to check for seasoning, adding more salt if necessary). Remove from the refrigerator, shape into about 30–35 round meatballs and set aside.

Place a large pot over a medium-high heat. Add the 3 tablespoons of olive oil and sauté the leek, celeriac (celery root), potatoes, carrots and bay leaf for 4–5 minutes. Pour in the stock or water, season with salt and pepper to taste and bring to the boil. Carefully add the meatballs to the soup, one at a time. Bring the heat down to low, cover and gently simmer for 30–35 minutes. Adjust the seasoning if necessary and remove from the heat.

Ladle about 250ml (9fl oz) of soup through a sieve into a heatproof jug (pitcher), returning any vegetables to the soup after straining.

Separate the eggs. Beat the whites into a light meringue, then whisk in the egg yolks, one at a time.

In a medium bowl, mix the lemon juice and cornflour (cornstarch) until the cornflour dissolves. Gradually pour in the

reserved strained soup, while whisking.

Now, slowly pour this mixture into the eggs, whisking constantly until smooth and fluffy. Pour it into the soup, place the lid on the pot and, holding the pot well with both hands to secure the lid, shake the pot to mix. Return the pot to the stovetop and turn the heat to low. Gently simmer for a couple of minutes, shaking the pot occasionally.

(This way you prevent ruining the meatballs by stirring it properly with a spoon.)

Serve with chopped dill and ground black pepper.

Baked rice pudding

Known as *rizogalo* in Greek (pictured on page 87), variations of this recipe are found all across the country. The baked version is usually served plain or with a citrusy sweet preserve or marmalade. Apart from the classic vanilla and cinnamon (and sometimes ground nuts), rice pudding is often flavoured with citrus zest, saffron, or *mastiha*, as in this recipe.

Mastiha, an aromatic resin extracted from the trunks of the mastic trees that grow on the south side of Chios island, has a unique flavour and natural medicinal properties. It is among my favourite Greek products and I use it a lot. Herodotus alludes to the collection and consumption of *mastiha* widely as a chewing gum (this is where 'masticate' derives from). Ancient Greek healers recognized the natural antioxidant, anti-inflammatory and antimicrobial properties and used it to treat patients suffering from stomach and digestive problems, as well as oral infections.

The method of cultivating *mastiha* on Chios has been preserved and passed down through the generations since ancient times, and in 2014 it was inscribed in UNESCO's Representative List of the Intangible Cultural Heritage of Humanity. The preparation for the collection of *mastiha* is called *kentos*, from *kentima*, which means embroidery – the specialists artfully 'embroider' (score) the trunks and large branches of the trees using a sharp tool and the mastic 'tears' drip onto the prepared ground around them. The 'tears' crystallize in about 15–20 days, and are then picked from the ground and thoroughly cleaned.

Greek cuisine uses *mastiha* in an array of baked goods, ice cream and sweet treats, but also in savoury dishes, such as sauces and stews. It is added to coffee and tea, as well as cocktails, while on Chios it is used to flavour a local version of ouzo.

If you can't find *mastiha*, replace it with vanilla, although the flavour will be quite different.

SERVES 6

60g (2oz) glacé[1] rice (medium-grain
  glutinous rice)
Pinch of salt
780ml (26fl oz) whole milk
2–3 strips of pared lemon zest (using
  a swivel peeler)
1 cinnamon stick
½ tsp powdered *mastiha*, ground with a
  pinch of sugar using a pestle and mortar
30g (1oz) cornflour (cornstarch)
1 large egg yolk, at room temperature
60g (2oz) caster (superfine) sugar
Ground pistachios, to serve (optional)

Rinse the rice, place in a bowl and soak in
cold water for 30–60 minutes. Drain and
put in a saucepan with 180ml (6fl oz) fresh
water and the salt. Place over a medium-
high heat and bring just to the boil, then
turn the heat down to medium and simmer
for about 5 minutes, stirring occasionally,
until the rice is partially cooked and there is
still some liquid left. Remove from the heat
and leave to rest in the remaining liquid.

In a separate saucepan, add 500ml
(17fl oz) of the milk, lemon zest, cinnamon
and powdered *mastiha*. Gently warm over
a very low heat for 5–7 minutes, stirring
so it doesn't bubble over, until the milk
is flavoured with the spices and lemon.
Remove from the heat and set aside.

Preheat the oven to 220°C/200°C fan/
425°F/gas mark 7.

Mix the cornflour (cornstarch) with the
remaining milk until dissolved. Whisk the
egg yolk in a separate, large bowl with the
sugar, until creamy. Pour in the milk and
cornflour mixture gradually while whisking,
until nice and frothy.

Strain the warm infused milk to remove
the aromatics, then slowly pour this into
the cornflour mixture, whisking vigorously.
Transfer the mixture to the pan with the rice,
mix with a wooden spoon and place over a
medium-low heat. Cook, stirring constantly
to prevent it from sticking, for 8–10 minutes,
until it starts to thicken but is still quite
loose. Pour the mixture into six ramekins.

Place the ramekins in a deep baking dish.
Pour enough hot water into the baking
dish to reach halfway up the sides of
the ramekins.

Place the dish in the centre of the oven
and bake for 25–30 minutes or until
slightly risen and browned on top. Allow
to cool slightly, then sprinkle with ground
pistachios, if desired, and serve warm, at
room temperature or cold.

---

[1] One of the oldest cultivated varieties of rice. Short-grained and rounded, and high in starch, glacé is ideal in rice
puddings and soups. It is quite sticky once cooked and highly absorbent, so it is also often used in pies, either ground
or whole, to absorb excess moisture.

FLOUR

Taramosalata with cuttlefish ink

One of the most iconic Greek meze dishes, *taramosalata* is a traditional dip made of salted and cured fish roe. The fresh eggs – from carp, hake, cod or flathead grey mullet – are generously salted and stored in barrels to cure, after which the cured roe is mixed into a paste called *taramas*.

There are two varieties of *tarama*: the off-white-beige and the pink or red one. The former is made purely of fish roe without colouring or other additives and hence is of much higher quality and better flavour. The latter contains less than 20 per cent roe, colouring, and often starchy additives and this is why its price is much lower. Pink-red *tarama* was invented in the 1950s in order to attract more customers with its appealing colour – the truth is that they succeeded, especially outside of Greece where often it's the only kind you can easily find.

Tarama and *botargo* were popular during the Byzantine era, with Greeks from Constantinople enjoying it as a meze dish along with other delicacies and cured fish. It became a dish associated with Lent and monastery fasting as fish roe does not contain blood so is allowed during such periods. The national day of *tarama* in Greece is on Clean Monday (Ash Monday), the first Monday after Sunday carnival, which is the official beginning of Lent.

Taramosalata would traditionally have been prepared using a pestle and mortar but nowadays most cooks will use a blender to give it an airy, mousse-like texture. I include a touch of cuttlefish ink here, which adds a hint of flavour and turns it a beautiful silver-grey colour. The most traditional way to enjoy *taramosalata* is with *lagana* bread (see page 184). I particularly love it with cucumbers, radishes and avocados. You can also use it in sandwiches.

SERVES 4–6 AS A SHARING PLATE
10 melba toasts (90g/3¼oz)
50g (2oz) white fish roe
4g (1 tsp) cuttlefish ink
1 small onion, roughly chopped
50ml (2fl oz) lemon juice
100ml (3½fl oz) sunflower oil
80ml (2¾fl oz) light olive oil
Extra virgin olive oil, to drizzle (optional)

Fill a bowl with water and dip each melba toast in for about 6–8 seconds to slightly moisten; don't let them soak too long or they will go mushy and this will make the *taramosalata* less thick. Place in a fine sieve to drain.

Spoon the fish roe and ink into a blender and pulse, in order to 'break' the eggs and release all the flavours. Add the onion and pulse until smooth, then add the drained melba toasts and lemon juice and blend until nice and smooth. Gradually start adding the oils while blending, to give it a velvety and smooth texture. Spoon into a container with a lid and place in the refrigerator for at least 30 minutes before serving.

Serve it as a dip. It can be stored in the refrigerator for 5–6 days.

Bobota, poor man's cornmeal pie with nettles

During World War II, in parts of mostly mainland Greece, corn was used to replace other staple grains that were harder to get hold of, such as wheat. Cornmeal pies became associated with poverty and variations of 'low budget' pies evolved around Greece, with small differentiations, often including greens or seasonal edible weeds and herbs, and sometimes a bit of cheese.

The use of nettles in Greek cuisine is common and can be traced back to ancient times. It is also a result of longstanding poverty and deprivation, which led people to make good use of everything at hand. At the same time, stinging nettles' medicinal profile has long been recognized, with Hippocrates listing 60 treatments using them, in addition to folk medicine that calls for nettle tea for the treatment of several illnesses including inflammation, hay fever, urinary tract conditions and arthritis.

For cooking, pick the young nettles that grow in spring – ideally before they grow too big and bloom, developing seeds on their tips. If you can't get nettles, simply replace them with more spinach or chard.

The pastry in this simple cornmeal pie is effortless and the result is light and, most importantly, delicious.

MAKES 12 PIECES

FOR THE PASTRY
240g (8½oz) cornmeal
120g (4oz) plain (all-purpose) flour
1½ tsp baking powder
½ tsp salt
120ml (4fl oz) olive oil

FOR THE FILLING
1kg (2lb 3oz) nettles
2 tbsp olive oil, plus extra for greasing
500g (1lb 2oz) spinach or chard, trimmed
  and roughly chopped
6–7 spring onions (scallions), including the
  green part, roughly chopped
5 tbsp chopped mint
300g (10½oz) feta, crumbled (omit for
  a vegan version)
Sea salt and freshly ground black pepper

Preheat the oven to 200°C/180°C fan/ 400°F/gas mark 6.

Wearing gloves, carefully trim the nettles by removing any thick stems, keeping mostly the top part with the young tips. Roughly chop them, wash them well, drain and blanch in boiling salted water for 2 minutes. Drain again, then rinse in cold water or an ice bath to retain their bright colour. Place in a colander and let them dry.

Place a large, deep pan over a medium heat. Add the olive oil and, once hot, add the spinach or chard, stirring until wilted. Mix in the spring onions (scallions), season with a little salt (remember the feta will add salt) and a pinch of black pepper and remove from the heat. Drain any excess liquid by gently pressing the spinach in a colander. Transfer to a bowl and mix with the nettles and the mint. Mix in the crumbled feta, if using. Adjust the seasoning if necessary.

For the pastry, in a large bowl mix the cornmeal, flour and baking powder and set aside. Pour 840ml (29fl oz) water into a small saucepan, add the salt and place over a medium heat until lukewarm, then remove from the heat and mix in the olive oil.

Brush the base and sides of a deep baking tin (pan), measuring 30 x 40cm (12 x 16 inches), with a little olive oil. Sprinkle over half the cornmeal mixture, ensuring it is evenly spread out. Using a tablespoon, drizzle half the warm water and oil mixture over the cornmeal. Do not

mix it or touch the cornmeal mixture in any
other way.

Spoon the filling evenly on top. Sprinkle
the remaining cornmeal mixture on top
and repeat the same process with the
remaining water and oil mixture. Bake for
50–60 minutes until a golden crust has
formed. Serve warm or at room temperature.

Tsouchti from Mani, pasta with cheese and egg

This simple dish is prepared in the region of Mani in the southern Peloponnese and is similar to the Italian *cacio e pepe*. Its name derives from the verb *tsouzo*, which means to sting, or to burn; in the region of Laconia where this dish originates, they use this word to describe boiled pasta that is dressed with hot oil or sizzling butter. The butter is crucial in this recipe as it adds flavour and texture to the sauce. Simple and quick to make, it is tasty and satisfying and calls for just a few ingredients.

SERVES 4

500g (1lb 2oz) bucatini pasta
2 tbsp clarified butter or ghee
100ml (3½fl oz) olive oil, plus extra to fry
  the eggs
350g (12oz) dried mizithra cheese,
  or ricotta salata, finely grated
4 large eggs
Sea salt and freshly ground black pepper

Cook the pasta in boiling salted water according to the packet instructions, then drain, reserving about ½ cup of the cooking water. Set aside.

Place a large, deep pan over a medium-high heat and add the butter or ghee and the olive oil. Let the butter melt and mix it with the olive oil. Once hot, add all but 50g (2oz) of the cheese and stir until it turns slightly golden. Add a little black pepper, then the pasta and a little of the reserved water – about half a ladleful – tossing the bucatini to coat well in the sauce. Remove from the heat.

Place a frying pan over a medium heat, add 2–3 tablespoons of olive oil and fry the eggs until the whites are set but the yolks are still runny so that they will coat the pasta.

Divide the pasta between four plates and place an egg on top of each portion. Sprinkle with the remaining cheese and add a dash of black pepper, if you like.

Pastitsio

The name *pastitsio* derives from the Italian word *pasticcio*, meaning a mess or a big mix-up (and from where 'pastiche' originates). The term was first used in Italy during the 16th century to refer to a category of hearty pasties that tended to be rather complex in terms of ingredients, and which included pasta and a variety of meats. They were prepared for special occasions, mostly to impress, which explains the use of the many different ingredients and the use of sugar – an expensive ingredient at the time.

Among the most famous is *pasticcio alla Ferrarese*, hailing from Ferrara, a city between Venice and Bologna. In fact, my grandfather's lineage is traced to this Italian city – his surname was Daferera, which was initially Da Ferrara before it was adapted to the Greek language. Family connections to the eastern part of Italy are not uncommon in Greece, as the Venetians occupied parts of modern-day Greece – particularly certain islands – between the 14th and 18th centuries. And vice versa, in the southern part of Italy, particularly Puglia and Calabria, where a lot of Italians have Greek roots.

The earliest records of *pastitsios* in Greece are during the 17th century on the Ionian islands, between mainland Greece and Italy. The one prepared on Corfu is very famous and is served at weddings, baptisms and other festive occasions, again as a way to impress.

The version prepared in most parts of Greece today is a baked pasta dish with a ground meat sauce, topped with a cheesy bechamel, without any pastry. Some keep the ingredients in layers like I do, while others mix the pasta and the meat sauce. Many cooks mix egg whites in with the boiled pasta and add the yolks into the bechamel, which makes it thicker and turns it a yellowish colour. However, I prefer to skip the eggs and keep it lighter. For the meat sauce, I use a sweet red wine instead of sugar. I use a Vinsanto from Santorini (a PDO-status dessert wine) or a sweet Mavrodaphne from Patra, but these may also be replaced by other sweet wines such as Port or Madeira.

SERVES 8-10
500g (1lb 2oz) Greek *pastitsio* pasta
　(or bucatini)
2 tsp butter, plus extra for greasing
8 tbsp grated kefalotyri cheese
　(or pecorino)

FOR THE MEAT SAUCE
3 tbsp olive oil
800g (1¾lb) minced (ground) beef (chuck
　and blade/shoulder if possible)
1 large onion, minced or grated
2 garlic cloves, minced
1 carrot, finely chopped
2 bay leaves

120ml (4fl oz) sweet red wine
400g (14oz) can chopped tomatoes
1 cinnamon stick
1 tbsp chopped parsley
Sea salt and freshly ground black pepper

FOR THE BECHAMEL
1.5 litres (56fl oz) whole milk
200g (7oz) butter
200g (7oz) plain (all-purpose) flour
⅛ tsp freshly grated nutmeg
3 tbsp grated kefalotyri cheese
　(or pecorino)

For the sauce, place a large, deep frying pan over a medium-high heat. Heat the olive oil and gently brown the meat. We call this process 'breaking' in Greece because what you are doing is cooking the meat and breaking it with a spatula until it looks ground and browned in the pan.

Add the onion and stir. Once the juices are mostly absorbed, add the garlic, carrot and bay leaves, and season with salt and pepper. Pour in the wine and mix, then add the tomatoes and cinnamon stick. Bring the heat down to low, cover and cook for about 15–20 minutes until all the liquid is absorbed. Adjust the seasoning if necessary, remove the cinnamon stick and bay leaves and mix in the parsley.

While the meat sauce is cooking, make the bechamel. Warm the milk in a saucepan over a low heat (do not let it boil). Place another large saucepan over a medium heat and gently melt the butter. Add the flour and mix constantly with a whisk to form a pale roux. Gradually add the warm milk, while whisking constantly, until you have used all the milk and the sauce thickens (you want it to be medium-thick, not too runny and definitely not too stiff). Stir in the nutmeg, remove from the heat and mix in the cheese. Season with salt and pepper to taste.

Cook the pasta until almost al dente (it is also going to be baked, meaning it will cook further). Drain and transfer to a bowl. Mix with the butter and salt and pepper to taste.

Preheat the oven to 200°C/180°C fan/ 400°F/gas mark 6.

Butter a large baking tin (pan) or baking dish, measuring around 35 x 25cm (14 x 10 inches). Spread the pasta neatly over the base of the tin (ideally in straight rows) and sprinkle over the grated cheese. Now spoon some of the bechamel on top (about 6 tablespoons), which will help the pasta layer set nicely.

Spoon about 6 tablespoons of bechamel into the meat sauce and mix to incorporate. Spread the meat sauce on top of the pasta using the back of a spoon. Finally, top it with the rest of the bechamel sauce and sprinkle with the remaining grated cheese.

Bake for about 30 minutes until nice and golden. Remove from the oven and allow to cool for at least 15–20 minutes before serving.

Orzo with mussels, saffron and ouzo

Orzo, which in Greek is called *kritharaki* (or *manestra*), is a rice-shaped pasta that is particularly popular in Greek and Italian kitchens. Interestingly, its name both in Italian and Greek means barley, which would once have been the most commonly used grain in this region of the Mediterranean. Research suggests that this kind of pasta was a substitute for rice, which as late as the 1960s was relatively expensive and hard to get. Orzo is used in traditional recipes, such as *giouvetsi*, where it is baked with meat, poultry or seafood. Its use is very versatile; it can be used in soups and salads, while these days in contemporary Greek restaurants, it is often used instead of rice for dishes like *kritharoto*, which resembles risotto. Here I make it with mussels, a common shellfish in the Mediterranean and a cost-efficient and easy-to-cook kind of seafood.

In this lovely recipe, I use fresh shelled mussels, as they make a far better broth, but frozen can be used instead. I add a pinch of Greek saffron for both colour and flavour; it pairs beautifully with the ouzo and the fennel fronds, which my mum often picks for me in spring from fields near the Athenian suburb where she lives.

SERVES 4

1kg (2lb 3oz) fresh mussels in shells
2 tbsp olive oil, plus extra to serve
1 onion, chopped
2 garlic cloves, chopped
2 bay leaves
Pinch of saffron threads
6 black peppercorns
2–3 cherry tomatoes
15g (½oz) sprigs of fennel
150ml (5fl oz) ouzo
1 litre (34fl oz) hot vegetable stock

FOR THE ORZO
4 tbsp olive oil
350g (12oz) orzo (number 1: large size)
1 onion, finely chopped
1 garlic clove, minced
2 tbsp finely chopped red (bell) pepper
3 tbsp chopped fennel fronds
Freshly ground black pepper

Clean the mussels, removing their 'beards' and discarding any that are broken or do not close when tapped on a work surface.

Place a large pot over a medium-high heat. Add the olive oil and sauté the onion until soft. Add the garlic, bay leaves, saffron and peppercorns, and stir for a minute. Add the tomatoes and fennel sprigs, stir for another minute, then pour in the ouzo and the hot stock; cover and bring to the boil. Add the mussels, cover and wait for about 5 minutes until they open. If you find any closed ones, throw them away. Using a slotted spoon, transfer the mussels to a plate, strain the cooking liquid and keep it warm. Set aside about 12 mussels in their shell for serving. Remove the remaining mussels from their shells and set these aside too.

For the orzo, place a large, deep pan that has a lid over a medium-high heat. Add 3 tablespoons of the olive oil and lightly toast the orzo for a couple of minutes until slightly golden (this will keep it from turning mushy). Using a slotted spoon, transfer the toasted orzo to a plate. Return the pan to the heat and add another tablespoon of olive oil. Sauté the onion until soft and glossy. Add the garlic and (bell) pepper and stir for a couple of minutes. Measure 900ml (32fl oz) of the the reserved mussel cooking liquid, add it to the pan and bring to the boil. Add the orzo back in and gently stir. Cover, reduce the heat to medium-low and gently simmer for about 15 minutes, checking occasionally and stirring, until most of the liquid has been absorbed. Mix in the shelled mussels and chopped fennel fronds. Season with pepper, garnish with the reserved mussels in shells, drizzle with a little olive oil and serve immediately.

Lioto me makaronia, slow-cooked lamb with spaghetti

Greek cuisine features a large number of lamb or goat stews and roasts. A lot of these recipes come from the islands, where goats and sheep are abundant and graze on the local greens and herbs, which enhances the natural flavour of the meat. These are simple recipes prepared with a few basic ingredients that locals have easy access to. Stews or slow-cooked dishes are also made with mutton, which is less tender and has more fat and a more intense flavour, making it ideal for recipes that call for slow-cooking techniques.

Lioto comes from Samothrace, an island in the north renowned for the 2nd century BCE statue of the winged Nike of Samothrace, and for its wild mountainous landscape with springs, streams and waterfalls. The dish can be made with lamb, goat or mutton. The plentiful onions melt into the flavourful sauce and, combined with the spaghetti, create a wonderful, hearty dish ideal for a special occasion. If you can't get nice, ripe tomatoes for this, use canned tomatoes with their juice.

SERVES 4–6

1 large or 2 medium juicy, ripe tomatoes
3–4 tbsp olive oil
1.5kg (3lb 5oz) lamb leg, with the bone, cut into portions of 180–200g (6–7oz) – ask your butcher to do this
800g (1¾lb) onions, chopped
3–4 garlic cloves, chopped
1 cinnamon stick
2 bay leaves
7 allspice berries
200ml (7fl oz) dry white wine
1 tsp dried marjoram
550ml (18fl oz) warm water
500g (1lb 2oz) spaghetti (I like to use number 5)
Sea salt and freshly ground black pepper

TO SERVE
Grated dried *mizithra* or ricotta salata
Chopped parsley

Preheat the oven to 200°C/180°C fan/400°F/gas mark 6.

Wash the tomatoes well and use a box grater to grate until you are left with only the skin; discard the skin.

Place a wide, shallow pan over a medium-high heat. Pour in 2–3 tablespoons of the olive oil. Brown the meat, in batches so you don't overcrowd the pan, turning it on all sides. Return all the browned meat to the pan and season generously with salt. Add the onions and garlic, cinnamon, bay leaves and allspice. Stir gently, then pour in the wine. Reduce the heat to medium-low and gently simmer for 2 minutes. Add the grated tomatoes and dried marjoram, remove from the heat and adjust the seasoning if necessary. Transfer the meat to a casserole dish (with a tight-fitting lid), then pour over the sauce and the warm water. Cover with the lid and bake in the oven for 1½ hours.

Meanwhile, boil the spaghetti for half the cooking time suggested on the packet instructions. Drain, mix with 1 tablespoon of olive oil and set aside.

Remove the lamb from the oven after its 1½ hours, and mix in the half-boiled spaghetti. Cover and place in the oven for another 10 minutes. Remove from the oven and serve sprinkled with grated cheese, chopped parsley and ground black pepper.

Galatopita, Greek custard pie

There are several traditional Greek desserts that feature milk as the star ingredient; most were traditionally prepared around carnival and Easter, or generally during spring when milk is abundant. Among the most popular of the milk-based desserts are *galaktoboureko* and *galatopita*, *gala* meaning milk. The former is syrupy while the latter is plain and lighter, and though both are divine, I have a slight preference for *galatopita*, which I highly enjoy with a cup of tea or coffee.

Most traditional recipes for *galatopita* call for sheep's or goat's milk, but cow's milk is used as well these days. What is essential here is the high quality and freshness of the milk as it will greatly define the final result, as will the butter and eggs. Some, especially in southern Greece, make this without filo (phyllo), resembling a baked flan; some in the north make it as an enclosed pie, while others, including myself, prepare it as an open pie, or tart. It can be served warm or cold, but always sprinkled with a little cinnamon and icing (confectioners') sugar.

SERVES 6–8

100g (3½oz) butter, melted and slightly cooled, plus extra for greasing
70g (2½oz) walnuts
½ tsp finely grated lemon zest
2 tsp ground cinnamon, plus extra to serve
60g (2oz) granulated sugar
7 sheets of thin filo (phyllo) pastry
(see pages 62–63 for homemade)

FOR THE CUSTARD

1 litre (34fl oz) whole milk
1 vanilla pod (bean) or 2 tsp vanilla extract
Pinch of salt
80g (3oz) granulated sugar
2 large eggs, at room temperature
50g (2oz) icing (confectioners') sugar, plus extra to serve
1 tsp finely grated lemon zest
100g (3½oz) fine semolina
40g (1½oz) butter

Generously butter the base and sides of a round 28cm (11 inch) baking tin (pan), 2–3cm (¾–1 inch) deep and set aside.

First, make the custard. Pour the milk into a large, heavy-based saucepan. Using a paring knife, slit open the vanilla pod (bean), if using. Scape off the seeds and add them to the milk along with the pod. (If using extract simply add it to the milk.)

Add the salt and sugar and place over a low heat until the sugar dissolves, giving it a stir every now and then and keeping an eye on it to make sure it doesn't boil. Just before the milk starts to simmer, take it off the heat.

Meanwhile, in a large bowl, whisk the eggs until nice and frothy. Add the icing (confectioners') sugar and lemon zest and whisk. Add the semolina and mix well to combine until smooth and creamy.

Remove the vanilla pod from the milk and give the milk a couple of minutes to cool slightly. Pour about 4 tablespoons of the hot milk slowly into the egg mixture, whisking vigorously. Repeat with another 4 tablespoons of hot milk, then pour the egg mixture into the pan with the remaining hot milk. Over a medium-low heat, keep stirring constantly until it thickens, about 2–3 minutes. Remove from the heat, stir in the butter, cover with clingfilm (plastic wrap) to prevent it from drying out, and set aside.

Finely grind the walnuts, lemon zest and cinnamon together in a food processor. Mix in the sugar.

Preheat the oven to 190°C/170°C fan/ 375°F/gas mark 5.

Lay the filo (phyllo) sheets flat on your work top. Brush the first sheet with melted butter. Carefully place it in the centre of the buttered tin. Sprinkle 2–3 teaspoons

of the sugar-nut mixture over it. Repeat with the next sheet, placing it crosswise on top of the first and sprinkling with more of the nut mixture. Repeat this process with the remaining filo and nut mixture, placing each filo sheet crosswise on top of the previous one, and finishing with a filo sheet.

Brush the top sheet with butter and pour over the custard. Smooth it out nicely on top. If there's too much excess filo hanging out of the tin, trim it, but leave enough to roll a rim. Fold in the excess filo, twisting and rolling it in to create a nice crust all around. Brush it with melted butter and bake on a low oven shelf for 40–45 minutes, or until golden brown on top. Remove from the oven and allow to cool down. Sprinkle with icing sugar and cinnamon to serve.

Tsoureki, aromatic Easter bread

My grandmother Evangelia is an exceptional cook, and I have recorded plenty of her wonderful recipes – this is one of them. Every time I make it, I feel so much pride in passing it on.

Tsoureki (pictured on page 105) is a very popular brioche-like bread in Greece and although it was originally connected to Easter, it is now enjoyed throughout the year. Its roots are traced to Jewish tradition and challah bread, and there are two main versions typically made: one simply flavoured with vanilla and orange zest, the other with *mastiha* (see page 84) and *mahleb* (see below). I go for the second version, as did both of my grandmothers.

Mahleb, which is one of the main spices used in this version of the bread, derives from the stone (pit) of black cherries, and is widely used in Armenian and other eastern Asian kitchens. Greeks inhabiting Anatolia and parts of Eastern Europe for several centuries meant that those Eastern spices were adopted by the Hellenic kitchen.

During Easter, we stick a dyed red egg (an old pagan symbol of rebirth) in the centre of each *tsoureki* and other traditional breads. In the Greek kitchen, all ancient breads that are either braided or shaped as a knot are symbolic, and these methods and shapes are meant to keep away bad spirits and negative energy.

MAKES 6

60ml (4 tbsp) lukewarm water
10g (⅓oz) dried active yeast
200g (7oz) caster (superfine) sugar
½ tbsp plain (all-purpose) flour
220ml (7½fl oz) whole milk
150g (5oz) butter
1 tsp *mastiha*, ground to a powder with a
   pinch of sugar (in a pestle and mortar)
1½ tsp powdered *mahleb*
4 eggs, at room temperature
Finely grated zest of 1 orange and 120ml
   (4fl oz) orange juice
1kg (2lb 3oz) extra strong white bread flour,
   sifted, plus ½ tbsp

TO FINISH

1 egg, beaten with 1 tbsp water
3–4 tbsp flaked (slivered) almonds

In a small bowl, combine the lukewarm water, yeast, a pinch of the sugar and the ½ tablespoon flour. Mix well to dissolve the yeast and let stand for 15–20 minutes.

In a small saucepan, combine the milk, sugar and butter. Place over a low heat and stir until the butter melts and the sugar dissolves. Remove from the heat and allow to cool slightly.

Mix the *mastiha* with the *mahleb* and set aside.

Pour the milk and butter mixture into the bowl of a stand mixer. Add the eggs, one at a time, while mixing on a low speed, until just incorporated. Add the orange juice and the yeast mixture and mix to combine.

Mix in the *mastiha* and *mahleb* and the orange zest. Gradually start adding the flour, mixing on a low speed at first. Once the flour is incorporated, mix on a medium speed for another 10–15 minutes. The dough should be soft, elastic and slightly sticky. Using a rubber spatula, collect all the dough from the side of the bowl and form a ball. Place it back in the bowl, cover with a dish towel and let it rise somewhere warm for 2–3 hours until doubled in size.

Line two large baking trays (sheets) with baking parchment.

Press the dough with your hand to release the air and divide it into six equal pieces. Divide each piece again into three equal pieces and roll into long ropes (about 45cm/18 inches). Plait (braid) three ropes

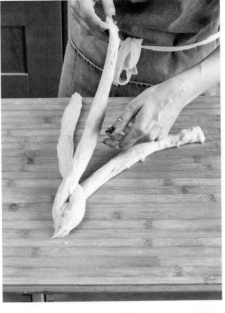

together, as you would hair. Repeat to give you six *tsoureki*. If you like, coil them into a spiral shape.

Place the loaves on the lined trays, leaving space between them. Cover with a dish towel and leave them somewhere warm to rise for 1 hour.

Preheat the oven to 180°C/160°C fan/ 350°F/gas mark 4.

Generously brush the beaten egg mixture over the risen breads. Sprinkle with flaked (slivered) almonds and bake in the oven for 30–40 minutes, until puffy and golden (see pictures overleaf).

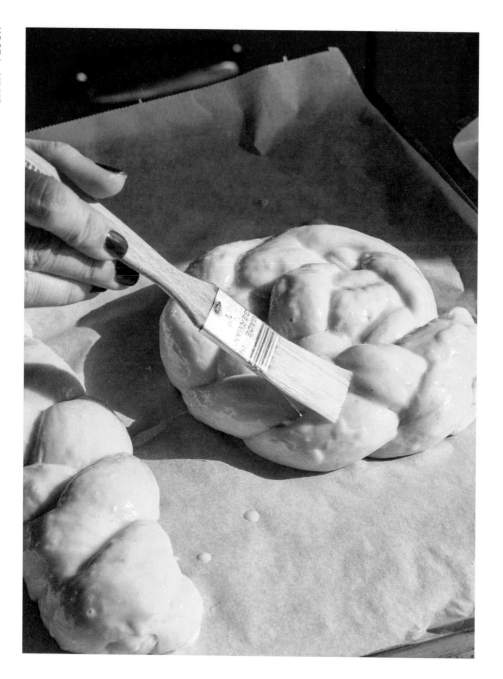

HIVE

Wonderful Creatures

There's something magical about bees and the way they coexist and work with nature. It is accurate that we call them 'worker' bees, as they are tirelessly devoted to their task like no other living being. In order to produce a pound of honey, bees must retrieve nectar from over two million flowers and travel up to 55,000 miles (nearly 900,000km). There are numerous varieties of honey with different textures, colours, flavours and aromas – even varieties that we categorize as bitter, usually with a very medicinal profile. The nature of a particular honey depends on the plants visited by the bees, the breed of bee, their physical condition and the environment in which they live, as well as other minor factors.

Honey is extremely nutritious, packed with all types of vitamins, enzymes, proteins, organic acids and minerals. Dark-coloured honeys (which mostly derive from forest trees rather than herbs or flowers) tend to be packed with strong antioxidants while at the same time they have a lower glycaemic index. Examples of such honeys in Greece are oak, chestnut and black fir tree honeys.

However, the quality of the final product depends in large part on how the bee-keepers treat the bees. The best honey is that eaten directly from the comb: raw, with minimum processing and a matched temperature to that of the hive, where the highest would be 37°C/98°F. Honey preserves all its natural nutrients as long as it is not heated above this; if cooked at high temperatures, it becomes merely a sweetener.

Yet the vital importance of bees is not just about honey production and the other valuable products we get from the hive; it is about pollination and the sustainability of nature, and the preservation and balance of our ecosystem overall.

The Symbolism of Honey in Greek Culture

Most of the symbolism and many customs relating to honey are rooted in ancient Greek tradition. On the one hand, honey is a symbol of purity – the unblemished, the sanitary – while on the other, it is a symbol of happiness, abundance, good luck and fertility. The ancient Greeks believed that honey was a god-sent gift that fell on plants from the sky like morning dew, collected by the bees each day. Ancient clay hives have been unearthed in areas around Athens, as well as other parts of Greece. Honey was commonly stored in amphoras and often it was mixed with wine and offered as a gift to gods.

It has always been a primary sweetener, and with much production nationwide, there has accordingly been great demand for its consumption. The ancient Greeks used it in sweet and savoury recipes, as a preservative or a sweetener. They combined it with fruit and cheese, baked with it, and mixed it into sauces, condiments and drinks. In the *Odyssey*, Homer describes *melikraton,* a drink prepared with milk and honey. Another common morning drink was *hydromelo*, lukewarm water mixed with honey, while every symposium would commence with a *propoma* – an aperitif prepared with wine or fruit juice mixed with honey.

Honey is still used as a sweetener in Greek cuisine and it features in most traditional Greek desserts, particularly those associated with festivities and happy occasions. It is poured over *loukoumades,* while *baklava* and *melomakarona* are both drenched in a honey syrup. Honey is also commonly served with cheese or included in recipes with cheese, such as pies and cheesecakes. The typical Greek yogurt is always drizzled with plenty of honey, while nuts or seeds are often caramelized in it and sometimes coated in sesame seeds. Honey is also often mixed into warm drinks, like in traditional herbal teas and alcoholic drinks such as *rakomelo*. At weddings, it stands as a symbol of fertility and bliss, and among common Greek wedding treats are walnuts mixed in honey, *diples* and *pastelia* (honey-sesame treats). Christmas and New Year traditions also feature honey, not just as an ingredient in the classic treats, but also as a symbol of good fortune. I particularly love an old Christmas and New Year's eve custom from central Greece called 'the feeding of the fountain', in which, at midnight, young women go to their nearest fountain to anoint it – 'feed it', as they say – with butter and honey, and often offer it other treats like wheat and cheese, wishing for abundance and a life as sweet as honey.

Hidden Treasures of the Hive

I am truly grateful for the incredible array of honeys I have tasted around Greece, and I consider honey-tasting a science as interesting and complex as wine-tasting. Eating a teaspoon with my eyes closed, I taste nature, smell the plant or herb at its core, and according to flavour and aroma, am inspired in different culinary ways to use it. It's a ready-made natural delicacy with such depth of flavour that it can elevate a recipe in many ways.

Greece produces many varieties of honey, from wild lavender or sage to eucalyptus and black pine tree. Among the most common are thyme, pine, orange blossom, mixed flowers, fir tree (black, red or white), chestnut, oak, heather and arbutus; each variety has its own medicinal profile and unique flavour. Honey is also used in skin products and remedies to treat skin conditions and wounds and it is widely used to treat coughs and flu.

The **honeycomb** is built by the bees in order to store honey and house larvae. It is made wholly of natural wax, produced by the bees in rows of hexagonal cells which are filled with raw, unprocessed honey. I usually buy the comb direct from beekeepers and at farmers' markets – it is pricier than a jar of honey, but is a very nutritious product worth spending that bit extra on.

The **beeswax** is very valuable, as the bees need both time and to consume lots of honey in order to rebuild it, which is why beekeepers tend to only sell the pieces that have naturally broken off instead of cutting chunks of honeycomb from their hive. Honeycomb is particularly nutritious, with antioxidant, antimicrobial and antibacterial properties. It is proven to be very beneficial for the heart (it lowers cholesterol), as well as for liver function.

The beeswax in the comb is edible, but some people prefer to spit it out after chewing it for a while. Beeswax is used in several other ways, particularly in natural cosmetics and candle-making. The candles are widely used in Greece, particularly in churches (probably because monasteries were involved with keeping bees), and they offer a wonderful natural aroma. The antimicrobial properties of beeswax also have a purifying effect when lit as a candle, making it an ideal sanitizer for small, crowded churches.

Bee pollen is best described as a vitamin bomb! Bees collect it from flowers and, in the process, pollination occurs. It is rich in proteins, amino acids, minerals and vitamins A, B-complex, C, D, E, H, K and R. It also offers anti-inflammatory, antiviral, antifungal and antimicrobial properties. Bee pollen is very beneficial for the immune system, metabolism and the nervous system, as well as liver function. I am a huge fan of bee pollen and I use it in several ways. As well as eating it straight from the jar, you can mix it into juices and smoothies, sprinkle it on yogurt, fruit or veggies, add it to salads or dressings, or even desserts. It is best not to exceed 1 tablespoon a day and, in order keep it fresh for longer, store it in the freezer. In the morning, I enjoy a simple juice of equal parts freshly squeezed orange juice and pomegranate juice, blended with a handful of mint leaves and a couple of teaspoons of bee pollen.

Royal jelly, also called 'bee milk', is a protein-rich substance secreted from the glands of worker bees. Larvae are fed it for the first three days of their lives, but the queen is fed it throughout her life. It is very difficult to collect, which is why it is something of a niche product. It is used as a food supplement and also in skin products and other cosmetics.

Propolis is a resinous substance produced by bees, who use it to seal and repair small cracks or holes in the beehive, protecting the colony from weather and other threatening conditions. At the same time, it keeps the hive sanitized due to its antifungal and antimicrobial properties. Another interesting use of propolis by the bees is that of mummification, which the Egyptians were inspired to copy as a method for mummifying humans. Propolis is used in natural medicine and you can either buy it in its raw form, which you chew, or as a tincture to dilute in water. It is also included in several health supplements and natural cosmetics.

A note on crystallization and storage

Honey never goes bad, it just becomes crystallized. This is natural and greatly depends on the type of honey rather than its quality. A forest tree honey, which has a lower glycaemic index, is less likely to crystallize (at least as soon) than a flower honey, which is higher in sugars. To bring it back to its original runny, clear state, you can gently heat it up in a bain marie (double saucepan) or in the oven, but only up to 40°C (104°F). It is best to keep honey in a glass jar, well sealed, in a dark and dry place, ideally between 5 and 15°C (41 and 59°F) and away from strong odours such as spices or garlic, as it has a tendency to absorb the odours.

Wild boar with quince, prunes and honey

Quince is used a lot in Greece during autumn and winter. Hard, sour and bitter when raw, when cooked the right way, with the right ingredients, it turns into a flavourful, creamy wonder that can be paired with an array of ingredients and spices.

The ancient Greeks gently simmered quince with honey, or honey mixed with grape molasses, resulting in something quite similar to quince paste. It was through this recipe that they realized quince would set when cooled when prepared in such a way.

As well as preserves and other sweet recipes featuring quince, traditional Greek cuisine often combines them with meat – pork being a classic that is often prepared during the Christmas season. I love cooking with quince for a festive occasion or winter feast, and one of my favourite ways is with wild boar instead of pork. Aside from being delicious, wild boar is a sustainable substitute for pork in Greece and many other parts of Europe; they have a fast population growth and tend to rip up crops and damage trees, including the very precious olive trees, so need to be humanely culled. The meat requires marinating and slow cooking. It's perfect for stovetop stews, but my favourite way is to slow roast it in the oven.

This is can be served with lots of options, from a simple rice or orzo, to mashed or buttery new potatoes.

SERVES 4-5

500ml (17fl oz) dry red wine
200ml (7fl oz) fresh orange juice
2 tbsp crushed pink peppercorns
1 tsp ground ginger
3–4 whole star anise
1 tsp dried marjoram
2 sprigs of rosemary
3 bay leaves
6 tbsp olive oil
1kg (2lb 3oz) boneless wild boar (thigh or shoulder; no skin), cut into portions of around 200g (7oz)
1 large onion, chopped
3 garlic cloves, crushed
250ml (9fl oz) hot vegetable stock
2 large quinces, peeled, cored and each cut into 6 or 8 wedges
1 tbsp honey
10 prunes, pitted
Sea salt and freshly ground black pepper

Put the wine, orange juice, crushed peppercorns, ginger, star anise, marjoram, rosemary and one of the bay leaves into a large glass bowl. Mix, then add the pieces of meat, which should be covered in the marinade. Cover and marinate in the refrigerator for 24 hours.

The next day, remove the meat and pat dry. Strain the marinade and set aside, reserving both the marinade and spices.

Preheat the oven to 190°C/170°C fan/375°F/gas mark 5.

Place a large, deep frying pan over a medium-high heat, add 3 tablespoons of the olive oil and brown the meat for a few minutes, turning it on all sides. Season with salt and pepper and transfer to a platter.

In the same pan, add another tablespoon of oil and sauté the onion until soft. Add the garlic and remaining 2 bay leaves, stirring for another minute. Return the meat to the pan, pour in half the reserved marinade and bring to the boil. Turn the heat down, pour in the hot stock and gently simmer for 20 minutes. Transfer the meat and juices to a large ovenproof casserole dish that has a lid, and place in the oven for 40 minutes.

Meanwhile, add the remaining oil to the same cooking pan you used for the meat, and sauté the quinces until golden on all sides. Add the honey and prunes and the remaining marinade (including the spices). Bring to a gentle boil and simmer for 5 minutes, then remove from the heat.

Once the meat has cooked for 40 minutes, remove from the oven, add the quinces, along with the liquid from the pan, and check the seasoning. Cover and return to the oven for another 50 minutes until the meat and quinces are fork-tender and the sauce has thickened.

Melopita, baked honey cheesecake

A type of ancient cheesecake was prepared on Samos island as far back as 800–700 BCE and anthropologists who have studied ancient cheese moulds unearthed in Greece conclude that some form of cheesecake probably existed even before 2,000 BCE.

This type of cake, or rather pie (as it is considered in Greece), was served as a wedding cake in parts of ancient Greece, with the bride offering it to the groom's friends and family as a gesture of hospitality. The actual ancient recipe survives in the book *Deipnosophistae* written by Athenaeus in 230 CE, and interestingly the ancient Greek method is not very different from today.

The cheese most commonly used for cheesecake is *mizithra*[1], but if you can't find it, replace the fresh *mizithra* with a creamy *anthotyro*[2] or fresh ricotta.

SERVES 8–10
Butter, for greasing
1.5kg (3lb 5oz) fresh *mizithra* cheese
260g (9¼oz) honey
1 vanilla pod (bean) or 1 tsp vanilla extract
5 large eggs, at room temperature
Pinch of salt
Finely grated zest of 2 small lemons
1 tsp baking powder
70g (2½oz) fine semolina
Honey and ground cinnamon, to serve

Preheat the oven to 190°C/170°C fan/375°F/ gas mark 5.

Butter the base and sides of a 27cm (10½ inch) springform cake tin (pan). Line with enough baking parchment to overhang the edges of the tin.

Drain any liquid from the cheese and place it in a large bowl. Mash it thoroughly with a fork. Mix in the honey and stir. Use a paring knife to slice the vanilla pod (bean), if using, in half lengthwise, and use the back of the knife to scrape out the seeds; set aside.

Whisk the eggs in a separate bowl until frothy, then mix in the vanilla seeds or extract, salt, lemon zest and baking power. Tip this mixture into the cheese and mix well to incorporate. Gradually add the semolina, stirring constantly, then tip into the prepared tin.

Bake on the lowest oven shelf for 45–60 minutes until golden brown on top. Take it out of the oven and allow it to cool. Once it has cooled down, remove it carefully from the tin and serve drizzled with honey and sprinkled with cinnamon.

[1] Made from sheep's and/or goat's milk and whey, *mizithra*'s production is very similar to Italian ricotta, which can be usually be used as a substitute. There are two types of fresh *mizithra* in Greece: *xinomizithra* ('sour *mizithra*'), a white, slightly granular, creamy cheese that is lightly salty and tangy; and *glykia mizithra* ('sweet *mizithra*'), mild and unsalted and used in several desserts. It is mostly grated.
[2] *Anthotyro* (also known as *Anthotyros*): A fresh, white, mild and low-fat, low-salt creamy cheese, made with whey and milk from sheep, goats, or cows, or a combination. It is available in dry and fresh forms, and has PDO status from several areas of Greece.

Melomakarona, spiced honey-soaked cookies

These lovely cookies are prepared all around Greece and Cyprus, mostly at Christmas. It was during the Byzantine era that they evolved into a Christmas treat, becoming particularly popular among the Byzantine Greeks and later the Greeks of Anatolia. The cookies are sometimes larger and stuffed – as my grandmother used to do – with a walnut half.

It is the temperature of both the syrup and the cookies that determines how soft they will turn. If you like them soggy, then the syrup ought to be cool and the cookies hot. If you prefer them firmer and crisper, then the syrup must be hot and the cookies cool. The time you soak them in the syrup will also determine the final result.

We always make a big batch of these as there are never enough to last through the holidays; they will be gone before you know it.

MAKES ABOUT 70
900g (2lb) plain (all-purpose) flour
1 tsp baking powder
Pinch of salt
250ml (9fl oz) light olive oil
260ml (9¼fl oz) sunflower oil
150g (5oz) brown sugar
½ tsp ground cloves
1½ tsp ground cinnamon
Finely grated zest of 2 medium oranges
50ml (2fl oz) brandy (ideally Metaxa)
160ml (5½fl oz) fresh orange juice
1 tsp bicarbonate of soda (baking soda)

FOR THE TOPPING
170g (6oz) ground walnuts
1 tsp ground cinnamon
¼ tsp ground cloves

FOR THE SYRUP
250g (9oz) brown sugar
1 cinnamon stick
1 tbsp lemon juice
4–5 slices of orange (with rind)
380g (13½oz) honey

Sift the flour with the baking powder and salt into a large bowl and set aside.

Pour both oils into a second large bowl and add the sugar. Let it stand for 5 minutes until the sugar starts to slightly dissolve. Using a stand or hand-held mixer with the whisk attachment, beat the oil with the sugar for 3–4 minutes on medium speed until thick and creamy. Add the cloves, cinnamon, orange zest and brandy and beat for another minute or so.

Pour the orange juice into a large glass or cup and, holding it above the bowl with the oil and sugar mixture in it, mix in the bicarbonate of soda (baking soda). It will froth and overflow. Slowly mix the juice into the oil mixture until incorporated.

Change to a flat beater attachment and add the flour in batches, while beating on a low speed. As soon as the dough becomes solid, I prefer to switch to kneading by hand as this helps me 'feel' the dough and knead it just enough to incorporate the flour. If you feel it is too oily, add another tablespoon of flour. Do not over-knead as this will result in dense cookies. The dough should look smooth and shiny and feel soft, not sticky. Cover with clingfilm (plastic wrap) and let rest at room temperature for 20–30 minutes.

Preheat the oven to 190°C/170°C fan/ 375°F/gas mark 5 and line three large baking trays with baking parchment.

Take a piece of dough about the size of a whole walnut and form it into an oval shape. Place it on a prepared tray, and continue shaping cookies until all the dough is used up, leaving space between them on the trays. Using the back of a fork, gently press each cookie on top and then lightly pinch them two or three times on the top (this helps the syrup to absorb). Bake for 20–25 minutes, until slightly golden.

continued…

Allow to cool down completely on the trays.

In a small bowl, mix the ground walnuts with the cinnamon and cloves. Set aside.

When the cookies have cooled completely you can start making the syrup. To a medium saucepan, add 300ml (10fl oz) water, the sugar, cinnamon, lemon juice and orange slices. Place over a medium heat and bring to a gentle simmer for 3–4 minutes. Remove from the heat, wait for 2–3 minutes, then stir in the honey until it dissolves. Cover the pan and keep warm for the spices and oranges to infuse further.

When the cookies are completely cool, place a couple on a slotted spoon and dunk them into the hot syrup for 20–30 seconds. Place each syrupy cookie on a platter and, while still hot and sticky, sprinkle with the ground walnut topping.

Loukoumades, crispy doughnut balls with honey

Almost every culture and cuisine around the globe has a type of treat prepared with a simple fried dough. Greece has plenty, which each have a long history. Among the most popular and loved are *loukoumades* (see pictures overleaf). These fried crispy wonders are either round or ring-shaped and they can be sweet or savoury, depending on the regional variation. They are always served warm and most commonly drizzled with honey and sprinkled with cinnamon. Sometimes sesame seeds or ground walnuts are also sprinkled on top and during summer they are often served with ice cream.

Make sure you use plenty of clean oil to fry them until nice and crispy, and adjust the temperature to keep the oil from burning.

MAKES ABOUT 35
250ml (9fl oz) lukewarm water
15g (½oz) dried active yeast
250g (9oz) strong white bread flour
1 tsp finely grated lemon zest
½ tsp fine salt
1 tsp thyme leaves
1 tbsp honey
1 tbsp lemon juice
Sunflower oil, for deep-frying

TO SERVE
Runny honey (thyme honey works well),
  to drizzle
Ground cinnamon
Lightly toasted sesame seeds

Pour 50ml (2fl oz) of the lukewarm water into a bowl with the yeast. Mix to dissolve and let stand for 3 minutes until it bubbles.

Sift the flour into a large bowl and mix in the lemon zest, salt and thyme. Form a well in the centre and pour in the dissolved yeast. Spoon the honey into the middle, over the yeast. Gradually pour in the remaining lukewarm water, mixing with a whisk or a wooden spoon until combined. Add the lemon juice and mix until incorporated. Cover with a dish towel and let rest at room temperature for 15 minutes until bubbles have formed on the surface.

Using a silicone spatula, transfer the dough to a pastry bag (if you don't have one, skip this step and leave it in the bowl).

Place a deep, heavy-based saucepan over a medium-high heat. Pour in enough oil to deep-fry, making sure the pan is no more than two-thirds full. Let the oil heat up to 175–180°C (347–356°F); test it with a bit of dough by dropping it in: it should sizzle and rise up.

Carefully pipe small, teaspoon-sized balls into the hot oil (alternatively use 2 teaspoons to shape the dough). They will immediately pop up and double in size. Don't fry too many at a time as they may stick to each other and the oil temperature will drop. I usually pipe around 5–6 at a time. Use a fork to swirl them around as they fry and adjust the heat when necessary. Fry until crispy and golden, about 3–4 minutes. Remove with a slotted spoon and place on kitchen paper to absorb the excess oil.

Serve warm, drizzled with plenty of honey and sprinkled with cinnamon and sesame seeds.

Diples, crispy honey rolls with walnuts

Diples are always present on festive occasions. They are made with a simple flour-based batter that is rolled out into extra-thin, sheet-like strips of dough, folded into a shape – usually a roll, bow or flower – then deep-fried. In fact, the name *diples* derives from the Greek verb *diplono*, which means 'to fold'. Tradition says that the more folds one makes, the more pleasant events will occur. When they are made at Christmas, it is said that they symbolize the swaddling clothes of Jesus, and the honey is for wellbeing and good luck.

For a simpler take, they are also fried as they are, without being folded or shaped.

MAKES ABOUT 18

5 eggs, at room temperature
1 tbsp sugar
1 tsp vanilla extract
½ tsp finely grated orange zest
1 tbsp ouzo (or brandy)
¼ tsp salt
430–450g (15oz–1lb) strong white bread
   flour, plus extra for dusting
Light olive oil or sunflower oil, for
   deep-frying

TO TOP

70g (2½oz) ground walnuts
½ tsp ground cinnamon
¼ tsp ground cloves

FOR THE SYRUP

400g (14oz) sugar
2 pared strips of lemon zest
   (using a swivel peeler)
400g (14oz) honey

Break the eggs into a large bowl and beat them with a whisk for 2–3 minutes. Mix in the sugar, then add the vanilla, orange zest, ouzo (or brandy) and salt. Whisk for another minute or so. The eggs should be pale and frothy.

Gradually sift in the flour, about 50g (2oz) at a time. Mix it in the bowl with a wooden spatula until it starts to get solid, then dust some flour on a work surface and knead for about 15 minutes until your dough is nice and firm and not sticky, nor too dry. Roll the dough into a ball, wrap it in clingfilm (plastic wrap), and let rest at room temperature for about 1 hour.

Divide the dough into smaller portions, about 200g (7oz) each, and shape into balls. Roll the first ball out using a rolling pin, until very thin (like making lasagne), or use a pasta machine on its thinnest setting. Using a pizza cutter and a ruler, straighten it around the sides, then cut into rectangles 9 x 20cm (3½ x 8 inches).

Place the cut pieces carefully on a dish towel, side by side, to prevent them from sticking on the work surface or to each other. Continue to cut all the remaining dough.

Line a large tray with kitchen paper and set aside. Place a large, deep frying pan over a medium-high heat and pour in enough oil to reach halfway up the pan. Grab two forks and keep them close to the pan. When the oil is hot (you can test it with a small piece of dough; it should bubble and rise up) carefully lift the first piece and place it in the pan. Quickly grab the forks and fold in the pastry from the short sides (see pictures, opposite). The dough should already look paler and bubbles will have formed. Quickly start turning the forks inwards, forming a roll. Fry, turning carefully and trying to retain its shape, until it turns golden on all sides and is crispy. Place on the lined tray to absorb excess oil. Continue with the remaining dough, placing the rolls side by side rather than on top of each other on the tray. Allow to cool completely.

Meanwhile, mix the ground walnuts with the cinnamon and cloves in a small bowl and set aside.

For the syrup, put 400ml (14fl oz) water, the sugar and pared lemon strips in a saucepan

over a medium heat. Bring to the boil, then gently simmer for 5–6 minutes until the sugar dissolves. Remove from the heat and mix in the honey until it dissolves. Discard the lemon strips and dip each *diple* into the hot honey syrup, turning it on all sides. Carefully remove and place on a platter or clean tray, side by side. When you have dipped them all, spoon a little extra syrup on top of the *diples* and sprinkle with the

ground walnut mixture. They will keep well in an airtight container for 5–6 days.

Note

If you want to avoid the rolling bit, you can cut them into pieces and fry as they are. Another technique is to cut them into squares to fry and press them in the centre to form a bow.

Portokalopita, orange pie

Oranges are a common feature in Greek pastries and sweets, and this luscious orange pie is among the most popular desserts. Some variations resemble more of a sponge cake and others, such as this one, use filo (phyllo) pastry. Rather than the filo wrapping or holding the filling, it is instead torn into small pieces and left to dry before being folded into a fluffy batter that is baked and then finally soaked in a syrup; the result is unusual yet lovely. Aside from loving the texture and final result of this method, I am particularly fond of the fact that this recipe makes good use of leftover and dried out filo scraps of all sizes.

Typically sliced into squares or triangles, this dessert is served either at room temperature or chilled, with a scoop of ice cream, plain yogurt, or just a dollop of whipped cream. Many ice cream flavours work well here, such as the traditional Greek *mastiha* (see page 84), a classic vanilla or chocolate or an almond or hazelnut ice cream.

SERVES 9

450g (1lb) thin filo (phyllo) pastry
(see page 62–63 for homemade)
200ml (7fl oz) sunflower oil, plus extra
for greasing
4 large eggs, at room temperature
150g (5oz) caster (superfine) sugar
Finely grated zest of 3 large oranges
1 tsp vanilla extract
¼ tsp freshly grated nutmeg
280g (10oz) Greek-style (strained) yogurt
(thick and creamy)
2 tsp baking powder
Ground cinnamon, to finish

FOR THE SYRUP

200g (7oz) caster (superfine) sugar
Juice of ½ lemon
1 cinnamon stick
6 cloves
½ orange with skin, cut into smaller pieces
4 tbsp honey (ideally orange blossom)
250ml (9fl oz) fresh orange juice

FOR THE CANDIED ORANGES

50g (2oz) caster (superfine) sugar
½ orange with skin, thinly sliced
into half-moons

First make the syrup so it has time to cool. To a medium saucepan, add 300ml (10fl oz) water, sugar, lemon juice, cinnamon, cloves and the chopped orange. Place over a low heat and bring to a simmer. Simmer for 2–3 minutes just until the sugar dissolves, then remove from the heat, add the honey and mix until it dissolves. Stir in the orange juice and set aside to cool completely, leaving the orange and spices in there to further infuse in the syrup. Once cool, strain and reserve.

Meanwhile, prepare the candied oranges. Combine 4 tablespoons water and the sugar in a pan and place over a medium heat. Bring to a simmer, gently mix with a spoon to dissolve the sugar, and arrange the sliced orange in a single layer in the syrup. Lower the heat and gently simmer for about 40 minutes, flipping the slices occasionally, until the rind softens and turns slightly translucent. Place the orange slices on a wire rack or baking parchment to cool down.

Using your hands, separate and tear each filo (phyllo) sheet into small pieces. They don't need to be perfect or even in size. Lay the cut filo out on a tray to dry for a couple of hours. If you have no time, you can dry them in the oven, at 140°C/120°C fan/ 275°F/gas mark 1 for about 10 minutes, but make sure they don't start to actually bake or go golden.

Lightly grease a deep (4–5cm/1½–2 inches) baking tin (pan) measuring 28 x 28cm (11 x 11 inches) with sunflower oil. Preheat the oven to 190°C/170°C fan/375°F/gas mark 5.

Break the eggs into a large bowl and beat

with an electric mixer for about 1 minute. Add the sugar and beat on a medium speed until the sugar dissolves and it turns frothy and pale. Mix in the orange zest, vanilla and nutmeg. Spoon in the yogurt in batches while beating on a low speed. Sift in the baking powder and mix well to incorporate. Finally, start adding the oil, gradually, while beating on a low speed. The mixture should be pale and very fluffy. Gradually fold the dried filo pieces into the mix, one handful at a time, using a rubber spatula. Pour the batter into the prepared tin and spread the top evenly using a spatula.

Bake on a low oven shelf for 35–40 minutes until nice and golden, and slightly puffed up. Remove from the oven and poke it with a toothpick here and there (this is to help it absorb the syrup). Start pouring the syrup over the hot pie, a few tablespoons at a time at first, allowing it to absorb. Once you've used up all your syrup, it might look too syrupy, but it will absorb. Let it sit for a couple of hours until it properly absorbs all the syrup.

Decorate with the candied orange slices. Slice into squares or triangles and sprinkle with a little cinnamon.

Pasteli, sesame honey bars with almonds

Over 6,000 years ago, the ancient Greeks prepared a kind of energy bar with honey and sesame seeds (hence the ancient name *sesamis*), which was offered to soldiers (including Spartans) for vitality; they are mentioned in Homer's *Iliad*, as well as in the works of Aristotle and Herodotus.

Pasteli (the modern Greek version of *sesamis*) has several variations: some are crispy, others soft and chewy, some plain or with added nuts and dried fruit or spices. The classic take on this recipe calls for white sesame seeds, but I like to mix in black as well as they add colour and flavour.

The traditional way is to roll out the hot dough on a marble surface, which helps it cool down faster and to harden without sticking to the surface. Not everyone has access to a marble surface, however, so I do it on a large piece of baking parchment, sprayed with orange blossom water, for extra flavour and aroma.

MAKES ABOUT 10, DEPENDING ON SIZE
100g (3½oz) blanched almonds
200g (7oz) sesame seeds
100g (3½oz) black sesame seeds
250g (9oz) thyme or orange blossom
   honey
1 tsp lemon juice
1½ tbsp ground cinnamon
½ tsp ground cloves
1½ tbsp finely grated orange zest
Orange blossom water, for spraying
   (optional)

Cut out two large pieces of baking parchment, each about 50 x 50cm (20 x 20 inches). Place one sheet on a flat work surface. You can stick the sides down with tape to prevent it from moving, if you like.

Place a large, dry frying pan over a medium heat and gently toast the almonds for 2–3 minutes. Transfer to a plate and, using the same pan, lightly toast the white sesame seeds, stirring constantly with a wooden spatula to toast evenly, until light golden. Mix in the black sesame seeds and remove from the heat.

Combine the honey and lemon juice in a bain marie (a heatproof bowl set over a pan of simmering water, or a double boiler) and gently warm over a low heat until runny, stirring occasionally. Do not let the

honey boil. When the honey is warm and liquified, mix in the cinnamon, cloves and orange zest. Fold in the sesame seeds and almonds, mixing with a wooden or rubber spatula, then remove from the heat.

If using, spray the baking parchment on the work surface with orange blossom water. Empty the contents of the pan onto the parchment, trying to spread it out as evenly as you can with the spatula. Place the second piece of parchment on top (you can also spray it with a little blossom water, if you like) and, using a rolling pin, roll it out as evenly as you can to about 8–10mm (⅓–½ inch) thick. Remove the top parchment and set aside. Using a sharp knife, score and cut the slab into diamond shaped pieces the size you want. Replace the parchment on top and let cool completely.

To store, either wrap them separately in baking parchment or clingfilm (plastic wrap) or store in a container lined with parchment. If it is hot outside and you want them to harden, store in the refrigerator.

COMB

Citrus salad with kumquats, honeycomb and pickled red onions

It was thanks to the Portuguese, in the 10th century, that oranges were more widely spread throughout Europe, and thus in modern Greek the named for orange, *portokali*, derives from the name for Portugal, *Portogalia*. Citrus fruit production in Greece has since become huge, and the fruits have many uses in traditional Greek cuisine.

Kumquats are a protected product of Corfu (PDO) and were considered a citrus fruit until the 20th century when scientists gave them their own genus, *Fortunella* (named after the Scottish botanist Robert Fortune who was the first to introduce them to Europe in the mid 1800s). They have a unique flavour, combining sweet, savoury and bitter, making them very versatile and a great addition to salads. When fresh, they are eaten whole, including their thin aromatic rind, which is somewhat sweeter than that of citrus fruit.

There is a bit of work involved in this salad, but it's totally worth it. If you can't get a good aged *graviera* cheese from Crete, use an aged pecorino, Manchego or even Parmesan.

SERVES 4–6

2 blood oranges, peeled
1 regular orange, peeled
2 grapefruit, peeled
1 small fennel bulb, trimmed, plus 2 tbsp
  roughly chopped fronds
100g (3½oz) lamb's lettuce
100g (3½oz) rocket (arugula)
6 kumquats, sliced into rounds (with
  the peel)
150g (5oz) aged *graviera* cheese from
  Crete, very thinly sliced
100g (3½oz) natural honeycomb, cut into
  small, bite-sized chunks (I use orange
  blossom honeycomb)

FOR THE HONEY-PICKLED ONION

1 large red onion, thinly sliced into rounds
180ml (6fl oz) white wine vinegar
1½ tsp sea salt
1 tsp black peppercorns
½ tsp coriander seeds
110ml (3¾fl oz) honey

FOR THE DRESSING

100ml (3½fl oz) blood orange juice
2 tsp white wine vinegar
Pinch of ground cloves
80ml (3fl oz) early harvest olive oil
Sea salt and freshly ground black pepper

The pickled onion can be prepared ahead. Place the sliced onion in a heatproof jar. Combine 180ml (6fl oz) water with the vinegar, salt, peppercorns and coriander seeds in a small saucepan. Place over a medium-low heat and bring to a gentle simmer for a couple of minutes until the salt dissolves. Remove from the heat, give it a minute to stop boiling, then mix in the honey until dissolved. Pour the hot liquid over the onion and allow it to reach room temperature before you cover with the lid. Chill in the refrigerator for at least 30 minutes before using (store in the refrigerator for up to 3 weeks).

For the dressing, combine the blood orange juice, vinegar and cloves in a bowl and whisk. Gradually whisk in the olive oil, then season with salt and pepper to taste and set aside.

Slice the oranges and grapefruit, or remove the pith to give clean segments, discarding any seeds. Set aside.

Thinly slice the fennel bulb, ideally using a mandolin. Place in a large bowl along with the lamb's lettuce, rocket (arugula) and fennel fronds.

Place a small pan over a medium-high heat and dry-fry the sliced kumquats for a couple of minutes, turning, until slightly browned on both sides.

Add two-thirds of the segmented or sliced citrus fruit, and most of the pickled onion, to the salad bowl. Add most of the kumquats, reserving some for decorating. Slowly add a little dressing and gently toss to combine. Mix in half the cheese and the honeycomb. Transfer to a platter, decorate with the reserved kumquats and remaining cheese and pickled onion, drizzle with extra dressing and serve immediately.

Tzaletia, corn and currant pancakes with apple and honeycomb

Greek-style pancakes, *tiganites*, are among the most ancient recorded recipes that survive and still thrive in Greece to this day. They were traditionally served for breakfast and made with olive oil, clotted milk, flour and honey. Over the centuries, variations evolved across different regions, and one of the most original takes are these *tzaletia*, which are often prepared on Corfu. What makes these different is the use of cornmeal, which turns them yellow.

Not only are these pancakes delicious, they are also quick to prepare. I top the pancakes with yogurt, honeycomb and spiced apples.

MAKES ABOUT 16 SMALL PANCAKES
200g (7oz) fine cornmeal, sifted
70g (2½oz) plain (all-purpose) flour, sifted
1½ tsp dried active yeast
Pinch of salt
1 tsp sugar
1 tsp finely grated orange zest
1 tsp vanilla extract
100ml (3½fl oz) orange juice
200ml (7fl oz) lukewarm water
60g (2oz) currants
Light olive or other oil, for frying

FOR THE APPLES
40g (1½oz) butter
3 dessert apples, such as Cox, peeled
  and diced
Pinch of ground cloves
½ tsp ground cinnamon

TO SERVE
Greek-style (strained) yogurt
Honeycomb, and honey (optional)
  to drizzle
Ground walnuts

In a bowl, combine the cornmeal, flour, yeast, salt, sugar, orange zest and vanilla. Add the orange juice and gradually pour in the water, mixing with a spoon until smooth and well combined. Your mixture will resemble a sticky paste. Cover with a dish towel and let rise in a warm spot for 30 minutes.

Meanwhile, for the apples, place a small frying pan over a medium heat. Add the butter and, once melted, add the diced apples. Mix in the cloves and cinnamon and cook for 5–10 minutes, stirring occasionally, until the apples start to soften. Remove from the heat.

Uncover the pancake mixture; it should have almost doubled in size. Stir in the currants. Place a large non-stick frying pan over a medium-high heat. Pour in about a tablespoon of oil and, once hot, spoon in a tablespoon of batter, pressing gently with the back of the spoon to give a flatter shape. Add another couple of spoonfuls of batter in the same way, no more than two to three at a time, and adjust the heat as necessary. When they rise and bubbles start to form on the surface, and they feel cooked underneath, very carefully flip them using a spatula. Cook for another 1–2 minutes on the other side, then gently transfer to a plate. Repeat with the remaining batter, adding extra oil in the pan when necessary.

Serve the pancakes with yogurt, and spoon some apples on top. Add a piece of honeycomb and drizzle with some extra honey, if you like. Sprinkle with ground walnuts and serve warm.

POLLEN

Lemony bee pollen and yogurt dressing

This wonderful dressing is perfect on a green leafy salad with fresh chopped herbs, and it can also be used to drizzle on fresh fruit; yogurt adds a pleasant creaminess and thickness. It is best freshly made, but if you wish to store it, do so in a tightly sealed glass jar in the refrigerator, for up to 2 days.

Fresh bee pollen is much tastier than dried and can be stored in the fridge or, even better, the freezer.

MAKES 1 MEDIUM JAR, ABOUT 250ML
  (9FL OZ)
60ml (2fl oz) lemon juice
30g (1oz) honey
1–2 tsp thyme leaves
80ml (3fl oz) extra virgin olive oil
70g (2½oz) Greek-style (strained) yogurt
10g (⅓oz) fresh bee pollen, plus an extra
  1 tsp (optional) to finish
¼ tsp chilli powder, or to taste
Sea salt

Combine all the ingredients in a food
processor and blend until smooth
and creamy.
  Serve the dressing with an extra sprinkle
of fresh bee pollen.

Tahini-yogurt trifle with figs and pomegranate seeds

This lovely trifle features some of the most important fruits in ancient Greece: figs and pomegranates. The ancient Greeks enjoyed these throughout the day: fresh figs for breakfast; fresh or dried as a dessert; and often as an appetizer, dried figs and nuts with wine.

According to Athenaeus, there were three kinds of pomegranate in ancient Greece: sweet, which they ate, medium-sour, and sour. The latter two were mostly used medicinally or to make vinegar. Pomegranates have always played an important cultural role that can still be found in Hellenic culture – as a symbol of abundance and fertility, wealth and good luck, life, death and rebirth. In Greek mythology, the pomegranate is also connected to important female goddesses such as Demeter, Persephone, Hera, Athena, Artemis and Aphrodite. Due to the myth of Demeter, Persephone and Hades, the pomegranate became associated with the cycle of the seasons, as well as a kind of symbolic link between life, death and the afterlife.

There are several traditions involving the pomegranate that are rooted in antiquity, the most significant that survives being carried out New Year's Day. In order to ensure a good and lucky year to come, people break a pomegranate on their doorstep. Usually, the chosen person is a child, whose heart is pure and honest, thus more likely to attract good fortune. After the chosen person enters, the rest of the family follows, always with their right foot first.

SERVES 4

30g (1oz) buckwheat kernels
30g (1oz) sesame seeds
1 tbsp nigella seeds
2 tsp ground cinnamon
30g (1oz) ground walnuts
4 fresh figs
300g (10½oz) Greek-style (strained) yogurt
40g (1½oz) wholegrain tahini
2 tsp Greek thyme honey (or other honey)
2 tsp bee pollen
4 tbsp pomegranate seeds

Place a frying pan over a medium heat. Once hot, add the buckwheat and stir for 1–2 minutes, then add the sesame and nigella seeds and 1 teaspoon of the cinnamon and lightly toast, stirring for 3–4 minutes, until the buckwheat crisps up and the sesame turns golden, and adding the ground walnuts for the last minute. Remove from the heat and set aside.

In a food processor, blend the figs. (Alternatively you can slice or roughly chop them if you want more texture.) Set aside.

Add the yogurt, tahini, honey and remaining cinnamon to a food processor or blender, and process until smooth.

Mix half the bee pollen with the buckwheat and seeds.

Get four small bowls and start layering. First add about a tablespoon (depending on the size of your bowls) of the buckwheat mix to each, to create a thin layer on the bottom. Spoon 2–3 tablespoons of the creamy yogurt mixture on top and spread it with the back of a spoon, creating an even layer. Sprinkle over about 1 tablespoon of pomegranate seeds and on top a couple of tablespoons of the creamed figs. Create a second layer of the buckwheat mix and repeat with the yogurt. Sprinkle with the remaining pomegranate seeds and pollen.

Blended spiced persimmon with saffron and bee pollen

Persimmon in Greek is *lotos*, which is a bit misleading when you are a child reading the *Odyssey* that describes enchanted lotus-eaters. I used to think that the lotus Homer was referring to was this fruit, so it became locked in my mind as a fruit that is so damn good, you lose your head when you eat it! Homer was definitely not referring to this fruit and likely meant the opium poppy; the ancient Greeks often used the phrase 'to eat lotus', when they meant to be absent-minded and forgetful. Despite my grand disappointment when, as a grown up, I realized that I had been totally misguided, there's still something inside me that believes in the magical powers of this delightful fruit.

Persimmons did not 'in fact' exist in Greece during Homer's time, although they are widely produced now. I use them a lot during their season – in both savoury and sweet recipes as they can be very versatile. My favourite variety is the Fuyu, which resembles mango in texture. The combination of persimmon, saffron and bee pollen is simply wonderful and I have experimented with those three ingredients in several ways.

I mostly use saffron threads rather than powder when I cook, but powder usually works best in recipes like this one.

SERVES 4

350g (12oz) ripe Fuyu persimmons, peeled and cut into smaller pieces
¼ tsp chilli powder
¼ tsp saffron powder
Finely grated zest of 1 lemon
2 tsp bee pollen, plus extra (optional) to serve
700g (1½lb) Greek-style (strained) yogurt
70g (2½oz) salted shelled pistachios, chopped

Place the persimmons in a food processor and blend. Add the chilli and saffron and pulse until smooth. Stir in the lemon zest and bee pollen and set aside.

Place the yogurt in a bowl and mix in 2 tablespoons of the persimmon mixture and 1 tablespoon of chopped pistachios.

Divide between four bowls. Top with the remaining persimmon mixture and sprinkle with the remaining chopped pistachios and some extra bee pollen, if desired. Serve immediately.

SEED

The Jewels of the Poor Man's Pantry

Pulses, the edible seeds from legume plants, have historically been associated with poverty and deprivation. They are traditionally looked upon as an affordable protein and nutritious 'stomach filler', as well as being a star ingredient in monastic cooking and other plant-based recipes suitable for Lent. With the rise of veganism and a global desire to follow a balanced diet, pulses have acquired a much more fashionable reputation. Greeks and other Mediterranean cultures have adapted their use in brilliant and tasty ways.

Historically, the most traditional pulses used in the Greek diet were chickpeas (garbanzos), broad (fava) beans, *lathouri* or yellow split peas (Greek *fava*), lentils, mung beans and lupins. The ancient Greeks used pulses in varying ways: as bread starters and flours, in soups, and even as snacks such as *stragalia* – the crunchy roasted chickpeas that are still popular to this day.

Lentils and, in particular, chickpeas remain star ingredients in many of today's ever-popular recipes: broad beans are used both fresh and dried; creamed Greek *fava* is a national favourite; and in the southern Peloponnese, lupins are preserved in brine and enjoyed as a snack to accompany alcoholic drinks. Native production and use of mung beans has faded over time, and they are instead now found in regions of the Peloponnese where communities are helping to preserve the local recipes.

Beans made their entry into Greek cuisine only after the discovery of the Americas, but they adapted well to both the local climate and to the hearts and stomachs of the people. Several varieties are produced, some with PDO status. The Greek national dish is a humble white bean soup, and beans are often also used in salads, or sautéed, fried, baked, braised, slow-cooked and more.

There are several traditional pulse-based recipes – usually featuring beans or chickpeas – that call for a small amount of meat (commonly pork, lamb or goat) to be added. This adds fat and flavour to the dish rather than offering a substantial meat serving.

During winter, soups with pulses are a staple in the weekly diet of the average Greek household. Lentil, chickpea and bean soups are particularly popular and nutritious, offering a unique sense of comfort and satisfaction at a very low cost. Trust me: with only a few good products and just three or four ingredients, you can cook a stunning dish beyond all expectations. There are three basic rules regarding pulses, which I live by:

1. They must be from the current year's harvest
2. They need to be cooked with plenty of onions
3. They need a good amount of olive oil added

In Greece, pulses are used in their dried form rather than canned; some require soaking overnight and some can be cooked without this step. I rather enjoy the process and anticipation of soaking pulses overnight as it kicks off my excitement for what I will cook with them the following day. An added benefit of soaking them in water is that it 'awakens' the seed's nutritional value.

Through the pulse-focused recipes in this chapter, I hope to offer a glimpse of the vast range of possible uses of pulses in Greek cuisine. Aside from teaching the different ways they are used in various recipes, it is also important to know how to combine them with other foods for optimum nutritional value. For instance, pulses should be combined with grains for protein intake and with vitamin C (such as lemon juice) for the best absorption of iron. From this humble ingredient, there is so much to gain, and I really do treat them as the precious jewels of my well-stocked pantry.

Nuts about Nuts

If you have ever visited Greece, you will likely have come across street vendors selling a wide selection of nuts and seeds – both salty and sweet. The nuts are sold in tiny paper bags: some are covered in sesame seeds and honey, some are coated in salt or other spices, some are plain and raw. They cost very little and are consumed by all ages with passion.

Greek cuisine sees nuts as a snack, something that can be traced back to ancient Greece when **walnuts** and **almonds** were typically served after dinner with wine, alongside fresh or dried fruit and treats made with honey, in what then was called *tragimata*.

Honey- or caramel-coated almonds and other nuts – often coated in sesame seeds – were very common and are particularly popular to this day. Another tradition that still survives is the stuffing of dried fruit, such as figs and prunes, with nuts. During ancient and Byzantine times, nuts were also used in sweet pies, mixed with honey and figs. Almonds and pistachios, the latter discovered by the Greeks after the expeditions of Alexander the Great, were widely used during the Byzantine era as a popular snack to accompany wine.

The symbolism of nuts (and generally all seeds) has remained the same for centuries, standing for prosperity, fertility and abundance. This is the reason most traditional festive treats, from Christmas to weddings and baptisms, feature nuts in some way. In some of these, the nuts are the primary ingredient; in others, they are simply a garnish. Almost all traditional Greek wedding treats – everything from drinks to cookies – revolve around almonds.

The cultivation of **pistachios** in Greece began late, in 1896, and the most famous Greek pistachios grow on the island of Aegina, near Athens, where every year in September (harvest season) they hold a big pistachio festival on the island. Greek pistachios, which have become synonymous with this island, have a beautiful pink skin and are bright green inside. They are extremely tasty and a popular snack – raw or roasted and salted. Fresh pistachios straight from the tree are a whole different story, and I have been a huge lover of them ever since I was a child, as my grandmother grew pistachio trees in her beautiful garden on Aegina. In old-school baking and pastry-making, they are often caramelized or used in different types of truffles, or as a garnish on top of syrupy treats. Wonderful ice creams are made with pistachios, as well as pistachio butter and tahini-based *halvas*.

These days, contemporary chefs are using them more than ever in both sweet and savoury recipes.

Chestnuts mostly grow on Crete and in mountainous regions. They are used a lot in winter and festive cooking, in recipes such as stews and stuffings. The chestnut tree honey produced in monasteries in Mount Athos is among my favourites – a truly exceptional product.

In recipes with an Eastern influence, particularly in rice dishes, the use of **pine nuts** is quite common, often combined with currants.

A type of very tasty oblong **hazelnut** that looks like an acorn grows in the northern region of Arta, and wild hazelnut trees are abundant in the mountainous regions of Greek Macedonia, Thessaly and Thrace. Hazelnuts are usually combined with chocolate, and although they have grown in Greece since ancient times, they are rarely used in old recipes.

Peanuts are produced mainly in Kalamata and Serres, often caramelized or added to energy bars or chocolate treats, and are used for nut butters.

Saintly Seeds

Like nuts, seeds have also always featured strongly in Greek cuisine, still carrying symbolic meanings from the past – namely prosperity and abundance. Seeds are used in breads and baked goods, in pies and sweets and in healthy treats.

Tahini is effectively a butter produced from **sesame seeds**, and both have long been staple ingredients of monastic cooking and traditional fasting periods. The richness of tahini and the high nutritional profile of sesame seeds have proved ideal not just for fasting periods but also for those following a vegan diet. Tahini is used in various ways – in soups (which I adore),

salad dressings and sauces. It is also used in breads and pastries and sweet treats like *halva*. Tahini *halva* is another classic Lent season treat, which was imported into Greek cuisine in the early 1920s via the Greeks who had settled in Asia Minor.

Those same Greeks imported and spread the use of **nigella seeds**, with their wonderful hint of flavour that reminds me of my grandmother Rena, who grew up in Istanbul and used them a lot in her recipes.

Aniseed and **fennel seeds** are widely used in baking, cooking and alcohol production, namely in ouzo, a type of *tsipouro,* and in digestif liqueurs.

Poppy seeds have been used for centuries and are found in the recipe for *gastrin* – an ancient Greek treat similar to what we today call *baklava.*

Leaving no seed unearthed, **flaxseeds** are often used in baked goods; the ancient Spartans were topping bread with them as early as 600 BCE.

Other seeds such as **sunflower** or **pumpkin seeds** are commonly enjoyed as a snack, especially while still in their shell – shelling them is a rather meditative process.

Carob is a seed that grows in a pod. Carob trees grow in many parts of Greece, particularly the south. Traditionally, carob – which has now made a comeback – is used in breads, rusks, crackers and biscuits. Apart from the gluten-free flour produced from the seeds, its syrup is also used as a natural, healthy sweetener, both in sweet and savoury recipes. It is often used as a healthy substitute for chocolate; it has a naturally sweet favour and is very rich in important vitamins and minerals.

Fava with marinated anchovies

There is often confusion regarding the Greek dish *fava*, primarily because what we call *fava* in Greek is not related to the more commonly known fava or broad bean. Greek *fava* is usually made either from a yellow legume, *lathouri* in Greek, or from a kind of pea often called *katsouni*. Both of these pulses have been grown in Greece and used in the Greek diet for at least 3,600 years. There are several varieties of *lathouri*, and those grown on Santorini have PDO status.

The pods are dried, then crushed (split), often still using traditional stone mills. The pea is named *fava* from the moment it is split and ready to use. Each kind differs in shape, colour, texture and flavour, with the best varieties considered those that grow on volcanic soil or in earthquake-prone regions.

Fava is easy to prepare, very nutritious and high in protein, as well as low in cost – all reasons that account for its popularity in Greece. It can be prepared as a soup during winter but most commonly it is served as a creamy purée. When different toppings are added, such as caramelized onions and capers, *fava* is called *pantremeni,* which means 'married'. It can also be made with other pulses as well, such as split green peas, red lentils or even dried and split broad (fava) beans.

Recipes vary, but it is always an easy dish to make, and pairs beautifully with fish, especially oily fish such as anchovies, sardines and mackerel, and other seafood, in particular grilled octopus and calamari. At home, I often like to keep it vegan and I serve it as a main dish with rice, olives and salad on the side.

Marinated fish and other seafood is a common meze dish, and for Greeks 'marinated' is a term used for raw fish and seafood that has been 'cooked' in the acid of typically vinegar and sea salt – similar to *ceviche*. Later it is preserved in olive oil with garlic, spices, herbs or other ingredients to enhance the flavours.

This is an easy recipe for marinated anchovies, but you must use very fresh fish. Alternatively, you can use store-bought or, if you want to keep it vegan, skip the fish. I add a little tomato paste to the dish to sweeten it up. And I 'marry' my *fava* with chopped tomatoes, onions and parsley mixed with capers and topped with marinated anchovies.

SERVES 4 AS A SHARING PLATE
250g (9oz) dried yellow split peas
  (Greek *fava*)
100ml (3½fl oz) olive oil, plus extra to serve
1 onion, roughly chopped
1 bay leaf
1 large garlic clove, roughly chopped
1 tsp ground coriander
1 tsp tomato purée (paste)
  (double concentrate)
600ml (20fl oz) hot vegetable stock
  or water
2 tbsp lemon juice
½ tsp dried oregano
Sea salt and freshly ground black pepper

FOR THE MARINATED ANCHOVIES
500g (1lb 2oz) fresh anchovies
1 tbsp flaky sea salt
450ml (15¼fl oz) good-quality red or white
  wine vinegar
1 garlic clove, thinly sliced
5–6 black peppercorns (or more to taste)
2–3 small sprigs of oregano
Olive oil

TO SERVE
1–2 tsp capers (rinsed if salt-packed)
10–12 cherry tomatoes, diced and drained
2–3 tbsp roughly chopped red onion
2 tbsp roughly chopped parsley

continued…

If marinating your own anchovies rather than using store-bought, first clean and fillet the anchovies: using kitchen scissors or a paring knife, gently cut around the head and pull it off, removing with it the entrails. Cut along the stomach, open in two, grab the spine and gently pull it out. You can leave the fish butterflied like this, or separate it into two fillets. Repeat with all the anchovies, and place on a large, flat tray side by side, skin side down. Sprinkle with the flaky salt and pour over the vinegar, making sure it's evenly distributed. Cover and marinate in the refrigerator for 2 hours.

Strain and wash the fish under cold running water. The fillets should have whitened and turned opaque (cooked in the salt and the acid). Place in a colander and let dry for 10 minutes. Arrange the fillets flat and side by side in a glass container with a tight-fitting lid. Add the garlic, peppercorns and fresh oregano. Pour in enough olive oil to completely cover the fish. Cover and keep in the refrigerator for up to a week.

Rinse the split peas and drain. Place in a bowl, add water to cover and soak for about 30 minutes, then drain and set aside.

Place a large saucepan over a medium-high heat, add half the olive oil and sauté the onion and bay leaf for 3–4 minutes until the onion softens. Add the garlic, ground coriander and tomato paste and stir for a minute. Add the drained split peas, stir, and pour in the hot stock or water. Bring to the boil and immediately reduce the heat to low (do not season yet). Cover with a lid that is ajar and gently simmer for 40–50 minutes, or until the split peas are starting to break up and the liquid is mostly absorbed. If the liquid has gone and the peas are still not soft, add a little hot water. As they cook, use a slotted spoon to remove any foam that may form on the surface. Avoid stirring the peas with a spoon as this will cause them to stick to the bottom of the pan. Once most of the water is absorbed and the split peas are broken down, remove from the heat and season with salt and pepper.

Tip into a food processor and blend until relatively smooth, gradually adding the remaining olive oil as you do so. This will give it a smooth, velvety texture. Finally, add the lemon juice and dried oregano, adjust the seasoning if necessary and mix well. As it cools down it will thicken further.

In a bowl, combine the capers, tomatoes, onion and parsley. Season with salt and pepper to taste.

Serve the creamed fava in a shallow dish, spoon the tomato and caper mixture over the top, garnish with 10 or 12 of the marinated anchovies, drizzle with a little extra olive oil and enjoy warm or cold.

Black-eyed bean salad

Simple, delicious salads with pulses and herbs, served either warm or cold, are common in Greece and black-eyed bean (pea) salad is definitely my favourite.

This popular pulse, which is native to Africa, reached Europe sometime during the 1st millennia BCE – probably during the time of Alexander the Great – along with many other ingredients. Black-eyed beans are easy to use because they do not require soaking and they cook quickly. They are also great cooked in a tomato sauce or stewed with spinach or other leafy greens (often edible wild weeds), and in soups.

I particularly like the combination of black-eyed beans and capers, and I often pair the two together, as in this recipe. This kind of salad is great on its own, but also works wonderfully as a side for grilled meats as well as grilled fish and seafood, which is what I usually serve it with.

SERVES 4

300g (10½oz) dried black-eyed beans (peas)
4 tbsp lemon juice
100ml (3½fl oz) extra virgin olive oil
3 spring onions (scallions), including the green part, chopped
1 small onion, chopped
3 tbsp capers in brine, drained
3 tbsp chopped parsley
3 tbsp chopped dill
60–70g (2–2½oz) spinach, roughly chopped
Sea salt and freshly ground black pepper

Rinse the beans (peas) under running water, place in a pot, add cold water to cover and place over a medium heat. Bring to the boil, and as soon as it starts boiling, remove from the heat and drain. Cover again with fresh water and place back over a medium heat. Bring to the boil again, add a little salt and simmer for about 30 minutes until cooked. This trick applied to any pulse will ensure it retains a good texture, which is especially important when using them in salads where you need them to be nice and firm. Drain and set aside.

Meanwhile, put the lemon juice in a small bowl and gradually whisk in the olive oil. Season with salt and pepper and set aside.

Add the beans to a large bowl and mix in the remaining ingredients. Pour in the dressing and mix well with a spoon. I like serving this salad warm or chilled.

Revithada, clay pot baked chickpeas

Ancient Greek philosophers and scholars referred to chickpeas (garbanzos) as 'rams' due to the fact that a chickpea has a cute little curved horn on top. The Romans, too, adopted this perspective, as the Latin name for chickpea became *Cicer arietinum (arietinum* meaning Aries). My son Apollo, whose zodiac sign is Aries, particularly loves this story, and chickpeas.

Greeks on the Cycladic Islands use chickpeas a lot in their local cuisine, in particular a small and very flavourful variety that grows there. The island of Sifnos is particularly famous for its chickpea dishes, especially chickpea fritters and a dish called *sifneiki revithada.*

Traditionally, this recipe called for rain water, due to the fact that Sifnos is a very dry island with a low quality of drinkable water, whereas rain water is naturally soft and turned the chickpeas softer and creamier. It would be typically cooked overnight in a wood-burning oven (which adds a smoky flavour), and a dough seal would ensure all the steam was trapped inside the pot, guaranteeing the chickpeas were perfectly cooked by daylight, into something between a soup and a stew. I have adapted the recipe for a regular domestic oven, but ideally it should be prepared in any kind of clay pot with a lid; if this is not possible, you can use a casserole dish.

For best results, bake at a low heat for 4–6 hours, but you can stretch that to overnight as well. Another way, especially if you are not certain about the quality of the chickpeas, is to first boil them until soft (about 40–60 minutes), then transfer them to the pot with the rest of the ingredients, using the water in which they boiled, and bake them in a 190°C/170°C fan/375°F/gas mark 5 oven for 1½ hours.

Don't hold back on the olive oil: it really is one of the secrets of success for all pulses, along with the onions. It is dishes like this one that prove simplicity always wins.

SERVES 4–6
400g (14oz) small dried chickpeas
  (garbanzos)
420g (14½oz) onions, chopped
½ tsp dried oregano
2 bay leaves
2–3 small sprigs of rosemary
150ml (5fl oz) olive oil
Sea salt and freshly ground black pepper

TO SERVE
Extra virgin olive oil
Lemon juice (optional)
Crusty bread

Place the chickpeas (garbanzos) in a bowl, rinse well and cover with plenty of fresh water to soak overnight.

The following day, drain and place back in the bowl. Add the onions, some salt, black pepper and the oregano and toss to mix.

Preheat the oven to 160°C/140°C fan/ 320°F/gas mark 2½. Place the chickpeas in a large ovenproof clay pot with a well-fitting lid, or a casserole dish. Add the bay leaves and rosemary and pour in the olive oil and 1.2 litres (70fl oz) water. Cover with the lid and bake in the oven for 4½–5½ hours; the longer you cook them, the creamier and thicker the result.

Serve with a drizzle of extra virgin olive oil, a squeeze of lemon juice if you like, and fresh crusty bread.

Gigantes, baked butter beans with spinach and chard

Gigantes (giants) or *elefantes* (elephants) is what Greeks call large white butter beans, due to their size. These are particularly popular in Greece and are mostly grown in the country's northwest region, famously in Prespes and Kastoria, both stunning lake regions with a PGI (Protected Geographic Indication) for giant beans. Another variety of these types of bean, also produced in the same region, is dark in colour, tasting similar to roasted chestnuts.

Typically in Greece, giant beans are baked; it's quite common to add sliced sausage, spinach or other seasonal leafy greens, such as chard and sorrel, along with plenty of aromatic herbs. The recipes that include greens often skip the tomato, with the beans simply baked in olive oil and lemon juice.

Most important for success here, as with most recipes featuring pulses, is the quality of the beans. I buy them dried and I make sure they are from the same year's harvest. The actual time they will require to boil properly always depends on their quality and freshness.

Serve this with some crusty bread and feta, if you like.

SERVES 4

250g (9oz) dried giant beans
  (butter beans)
1 bay leaf
250ml (9fl oz) olive oil, plus 3 tbsp
1 large onion, roughly chopped
1 leek, halved lengthwise and thinly sliced
200g (7oz) fennel bulb, roughly chopped
1 tsp ground coriander
2 garlic cloves, crushed
5 spring onions (scallions), including the
  green part, chopped
500g (1lb 2oz) spinach, trimmed
  and roughly chopped (or left whole
  if not too big)
200g (7oz) Swiss chard, trimmed and
  roughly chopped
Juice of 1 lemon (or more to taste)
2 tbsp chopped dill
2 tbsp chopped parsley
Sea salt and freshly ground black pepper

Soak the beans overnight in plenty of water. The next day, drain and place in a large pot. Cover with cold water and bring to the boil. Remove from the heat, drain and cover again with plenty of fresh water. Return to the heat, add a little salt and the bay leaf, and bring to a gentle boil. Simmer for 40–60 minutes or until the beans are tender but not overcooked. Drain, reserving 160ml (5½fl oz) of the cooking water.

While the beans are cooking, place a large pan over a medium-high heat. Add the 3 tablespoons of olive oil and sauté the onion, leek and fennel. Season with salt and pepper and stir in the ground coriander. Cook, stirring, until everything begins to soften. Add the garlic and spring onions (scallions) and stir for another minute. Mix in the spinach and chard, adding in batches in order to wilt them down before adding the next. Adjust the seasoning and spoon the contents of the pan into the base of a deep baking tin (pan) or dish, making sure you scrape everything from the pan.

Preheat the oven to 200°C/180°C fan/ 400°F/gas mark 6.

Season the drained beans with salt and pepper and arrange them on top of the greens. Pour in the reserved cooking water from the beans and 80ml (2¾fl oz) of the olive oil, cover and bake in the oven for 20–30 minutes until the sauce has thickened. Uncover, mix in the remaining olive oil, the lemon juice and chopped herbs, then return to the oven, uncovered, for another 15 minutes or until they look almost caramelized. Remove from the oven, cover and let them rest for 15 minutes before serving.

Grilled octopus on lentils

At first glance, the lentils here may seem overshadowed by the grilled octopus, but in fact they bring a perfect balance to the flavours and textures of this dish. Both lentils and octopus have featured prominently in the Greek diet for many centuries. Lentils are still among the most staple pulses – a humble, affordable food that Greeks particularly love.

Octopus, on the other hand, has become a kind of stereotype of Greek island holidays and a typical image captured on postcards. Iconic lines of octopuses on ropes outside seaside restaurants, drying in the sun, have become part of the anticipated décor. To be absolutely honest, although I generally dislike stereotypes, fresh and sun-dried octopus grilled over charcoals is undeniably delicious, especially when enjoyed by the seaside.

I have been lucky enough in my life to have been able to spend long summers on islands. My connection to the sea and the serene island lifestyle has grown hugely throughout my life and I have come to understand that each island offers a whole different story. As a result, I have learned a lot of cooking tips for fish and seafood from fishermen and islanders I have met along my way.

A fuss-free way to achieve tender and delicious grilled octopus is to first boil it, a process that also has its grand secrets. The correct way, as taught to me by my grandfather, is not to add any water at all. Instead, you must let it boil in its own water. The water constitution of octopus is about 70 per cent, which means it already has more than enough flavourful water to cook in. It is also already salted from the sea water, so needs no extra salt. This, for me, is the one and only method for cooking octopus; it keeps its appearance and texture, and has a fuller and better taste.

Your pot needs to be very hot before you introduce the octopus in order to help it release its water. The cooking time can fluctuate, but generally speaking an octopus of around 1–1.5kg (2lb 3oz–3lb 5oz) requires around 40 minutes of cooking on a low heat. Boiled octopus can be kept for about a week if stored properly – cut it into bite-sized pieces and place in a glass container that can be fully sealed with a lid. Cover in olive oil and add in a bay leaf, a sprig of oregano, and a few peppercorns and you are all set.

continued…

SERVES 4–6 AS A SHARING DISH
1 octopus, about 1kg (2lb 3oz), fresh or
   frozen, cleaned and ready to cook
1 bay leaf
3–4 black peppercorns
1 tbsp red wine vinegar

FOR THE LENTILS
200g (7oz) small brown lentils
1 bay leaf
1 garlic clove, peeled
2–3 spring onions (scallions), including the
   green part, chopped
12 cherry tomatoes, diced
½ cucumber, peeled, deseeded and diced
1 tsp dried oregano, plus extra to serve
3 tbsp chopped parsley
70ml (2½fl oz) early harvest olive oil, plus
   extra to serve
1½ tbsp lemon juice
Salt

Rinse the lentils and tip them into a medium-sized pan. Cover with water and place over a medium-high heat. As soon as it starts to boil, remove from the heat and drain. Return the lentils to the pan and refill the pan with fresh water. (This way the lentils will keep their shape and texture better after they boil.) Add the bay leaf, a little salt and the garlic and bring to the boil. Lower the heat to medium and gently simmer for about 20 minutes, or until tender but firm enough to hold their shape. Drain.

If using frozen octopus, let it defrost completely and bring it to room temperature before you cook it.

Drain the washed octopus in a colander. Place a heavy-based pot over a medium-high heat. Once hot, put in the octopus, bay leaf, peppercorns and vinegar. Cover immediately and reduce the heat to low. Gently simmer in its own juice, covered, for about 40 minutes or until tender when pierced with a fork (to make sure, cut a small piece and try it). Remove from the heat and set aside. The remaining liquid in the pot can be used for seafood risotto and pasta dishes.

Combine the lentils, spring onions (scallions), tomatoes, cucumber, dried oregano and parsley in a serving dish. Add salt and pepper to taste, the olive oil and lemon juice, and mix with a spoon.

Cut the octopus into tentacles. Place a non-stick griddle pan over a medium-high heat. Place each tentacle on the hot pan. Cook for 2–3 minutes on each side, or until it looks slightly charred. You can cut the tentacles into smaller pieces and mix them in the lentil salad, or leave them whole and garnish the top of the lentils. Drizzle with a bit of early harvest olive oil on top and sprinkle with dried oregano.

Slow-cooked beans with pork ribs

Beans are a filling and low-cost ingredient and often a kind of universal symbol of a poor man's kitchen. This is likely why around the late 1930s, when most people were deprived of meat due to consecutive wars, the national dish of Greece became a simple, humble white bean soup named *fasolada* – an absolutely wonderful winter dish when properly cooked.

Greek *fasolada* is sometimes cooked with meat, usually pork – a small amount to add flavour and a bit of extra fat. It's not about the quantity – in the past many could not afford meat for their daily diet – it's about the flavour and the goal of feeling full for longer.

In this recipe I combine the typical flavours of a classic *fasolada*, but I slow-cook it in the oven into a drier dish (not as a soup). The recipe requires time to slow-cook properly until the meat falls off the bone. A hearty winter dish that pairs beautifully with red wine.

SERVES 4

250g (9oz) dried cannellini beans
1 bay leaf
1kg (2lb 3oz) baby back pork ribs,
  each cut into 2 or 3 pieces
½ tsp garlic powder
1 tsp smoked paprika
3 tbsp olive oil, plus extra (optional)
  to serve
1 large onion, roughly chopped
4 garlic cloves, crushed
1 celery stick, chopped
7–8 sun-dried tomatoes, quartered
½ red (bell) pepper, roughly chopped
⅓ tsp chilli flakes (or more depending
  on how spicy you like it)
2 tbsp tomato purée (paste)
2 tbsp balsamic vinegar
2 tbsp grape molasses (grape syrup)
1½ tsp dried marjoram
150ml (5fl oz) red wine
250ml (9fl oz) hot vegetable stock
Sea salt and freshly ground black pepper

Soak the beans overnight in plenty of water. The next day, drain the beans and place in a pot. Cover with cold water and place over a medium-high heat. Bring to the boil, cook for 2–3 minutes, remove from the heat and drain. Cover with fresh water again, place back on the stovetop over a medium heat, add a little salt and the bay leaf and simmer gently for 40–45 until the beans are done but not too soft and mushy. Drain and set aside.

Season the ribs with salt, black pepper, the garlic powder and smoked paprika. Place a large frying pan over a medium-high heat. Add the olive oil and brown the ribs, turning them on all sides for about 15 minutes. Transfer to a platter.

Turn the heat down to medium and in the same pan with the drippings (if necessary, add another tablespoon olive oil), sauté together the onion, garlic, celery, sun-dried tomatoes and red (bell) pepper. Season with salt and pepper, add the chilli flakes and stir over a medium heat until the vegetables start to soften. Mix in the tomato purée (paste) and pour in the balsamic vinegar and grape molasses (syrup). Mix in the drained beans and marjoram and pour in the wine. Give it a few minutes for the alcohol to evaporate, then add the hot stock. Gently simmer for about 10–15 minutes until the sauce starts to thicken.

Preheat the oven to 190°C/170°C fan/375°F/gas mark 5.

Transfer the beans to a casserole dish that has a lid, place the pork on top, cover and bake on the middle shelf of the oven for about 1 hour. Lower the heat to 120°C/100°C fan/250°F/gas ½, and continue to bake for another 40–50 minutes. Uncover and bake for another 15–20 minutes until it looks almost caramelized. Remove from the oven and drizzle with a little olive oil, if desired.

NUT

Roasted beetroot with pistachio *skordalia*

Skordo, which in Greek means garlic, has been at the core of the Greek diet for thousands of years. Aside from the fact that it was a staple food, especially for the lower classes, ancient Greek physicians such as Hippocrates and Galen considered garlic a valuable medicine, using it in their treatments and recommending it in the daily diet. Garlic was widely used in ancient Greek cooking as the variety of ingredients was rather limited, and two popular traditional garlic-based sauces were *skorothalmo* and *mittotos*. The latter became particularly popular as an accompaniment to cured fish, another ancient Greek trend. Both are considered predecessors of what we today call *skordalia* or *aliada*, a thick, creamy sauce or dip prepared with garlic mixed with a thickening agent and olive oil.

It can be made in different ways, with boiled potatoes or the classic stale bread, with or without the addition of nuts, usually walnuts. The traditional method required a pestle and mortar, but these days it's usually made in a food processor.

The tradition of serving a garlic sauce with fish never faded; in fact, the most popular way to serve *skordalia*, apart from alongside vegetables, is still with fried fish or other seafood such as calamari and mussels. Each year on 25 March, the celebration of Greek Independence and the Annunciation of the Virgin Mary, the national dish enjoyed all across Greece is fried salted cod served with *skordalia* and beetroot (beet). The combination is magical.

This recipe uses pistachios which, apart from lending a lovely flavour, also add a beautiful green colour. You can serve this dish as a starter, but to be honest, I often have it as a main at home, served warm. It can be served with any roast, fried, or boiled vegetable, and it's particularly good with fried or grilled fish and seafood.

SERVES 4

6 small/medium-sized beetroots (beets)

FOR THE PISTACHIO *SKORDALIA*

100g (3½oz) stale white bread (no crusts)
100g (3½oz) raw, shelled and unsalted
  pistachios, plus 1 tbsp roasted, salted
  pistachios, roughly chopped, to finish
3–5 garlic cloves (depending on size),
  peeled
1½ tbsp white wine vinegar
80ml (3fl oz) extra virgin olive oil
½ tsp finely grated lemon zest (optional)
Salt

Preheat the oven to 200°C/180°C fan/
400°F/gas mark 6.

Wash the beetroot (beets) thoroughly, scrubbing them. Leave them whole as they are, skin on. Wrap them individually in foil, arrange them on a baking tray and bake for 50–60 minutes until cooked through. They should be easy to pierce with a fork. Allow to cool for 10–15 minutes, then carefully peel them, wearing gloves if you want to avoid staining your hands. Cut them into wedges or smaller pieces and arrange on a platter.

For the skordalia, soak the bread in a little water for 5 minutes. Strain it, squeezing well, and set aside.

Place the raw pistachios in a food processor and finely grind. Add the garlic, vinegar and salt to taste, and process to form a paste. Add the squeezed out bread and process again until smooth. Gradually add the olive oil while processing, to give it a nice, creamy texture. Add the lemon zest, if using, and mix well with a spoon. The final result should be relatively smooth and thick as a dip. Serve, with the beetroot, in a plate or bowl, sprinkled with the chopped roasted pistachios.

Lagoto, braised rabbit in a tomato and walnut *skordalia* sauce

This is a traditional dish from the mountainous region of Arcadia in the central and eastern part of the Peloponnese, a pastoral place that has inspired ancient poets and many Renaissance artists. The area is particularly stunning and green and the nature is wild, with beautiful stone-built historic villages scattered around the slopes.

Some of the best honey and apples, potatoes and a variety of long and narrow aubergine (eggplant), as well as some of the most wonderful walnuts are produced there.

A walnut *skordalia* is used in this recipe, with the creamed walnuts and garlic mixed into the tomato sauce in order to thicken it and make it luscious and flavourful. Original recipes for *lagoto* use hare, but were probably prepared with other game and possibly cooked in this rich garlic sauce as a way to preserve it for longer. These days, it is commonly prepared with rabbit, pork or veal, and even fish.

This dish is typically served with hand-cut fried potatoes or pasta; I also love it with rice.

SERVES 4-6

1 rabbit, about 1.2kg (2lb 10oz), cut into
  8 portions
3 tbsp vinegar
5 tbsp olive oil
1 onion, chopped
3 bay leaves
1 cinnamon stick
5 cloves
150ml (5fl oz) dry red wine
600g (1lb 5oz) canned chopped tomatoes
380–400ml (13–14fl oz) warm water
Sea salt and freshly ground black pepper

FOR THE WALNUT *SKORDALIA*

100g (3½oz) stale white bread (no crusts)
100g (3½oz) walnuts
3-5 garlic cloves (depending on size),
  peeled
½ tsp salt
2 tbsp red wine vinegar
70ml (2½fl oz) olive oil

Wash the rabbit with water, drain and place in a bowl with the vinegar. Rub it with the vinegar and let it sit for 10 minutes. Wash it again and drain. Pat dry with kitchen paper and set aside.

Place a large, wide pan that has a tight-fitting lid over a medium-high heat. Once hot, pour in 3 tablespoons of the olive oil and brown the rabbit pieces, turning on all sides. Transfer to a platter. Pour the remaining 2 tablespoons of olive oil into the same pan and sauté the onion and bay leaves for a couple of minutes over a medium heat. Return the meat to the pan, add the cinnamon and cloves, season with salt and pepper and pour in the wine, letting the alcohol evaporate for a couple of minutes. Add the chopped tomatoes and pour in enough of the warm water to just cover the meat. Cover with the lid, turn the heat down to medium-low and gently braise for about 50 minutes.

Meanwhile, soak the bread in a little water for 5 minutes. Drain it well, squeezing it between your hands, and set aside. Place the walnuts in a food processor and finely grind. Add the garlic, salt and vinegar, and process well. Add the soaked, squeezed out bread and process until smooth. Gradually add the olive oil while processing; the *skordalia* should be relatively smooth and thick.

Take the lid off the rabbit pan and let it simmer for 5-7 minutes. Lower the heat and mix in the walnut *skordalia*. Gently simmer for 10 minutes until the sauce looks thick and creamy. Adjust the seasoning, if necessary, then remove from the heat and let the *lagoto* sit, uncovered, for 10-15 minutes before serving.

Veal cheeks and chestnut *stifado* with creamed celeriac

This sort of dish entered Greek kitchens during the 13th century Venetian rule of several parts of, mostly southern, Greece. The word *stifado* itself comes from the ancient Greek word *tyfos*, meaning steam, from which the Latin word *estufare* is rooted, and thus where the Italian word for stew – *stufato* (or Venetian *stufado*) – was born.

As the name suggests, *stifado* is a stew, usually involving meat, commonly hare or rabbit, veal or beef, and often octopus. The version here combines my love for veal cheeks with the Cretan influence of adding chestnuts. The veal cheeks are cooked until fork-tender and the chestnuts caramelize along with the pearl onions. I serve it over a velvety celeriac (celery root) purée, with plenty of sauce, and the result is so festive and delicious that I often cook it on New Year's Day. It is possible to replace the veal cheeks with another cut of beef or veal appropriate for stews, but I would highly recommend trying it with cheeks.

SERVES 4

FOR THE *STIFADO*
750g (1lb 10½oz) pearl onions
120ml (4fl oz) olive oil
800g (1¾lb) veal cheeks with fat trimmed
  off (ask your butcher to do it) and,
  depending on size, cut into about 7cm
  (2¾ inch) chunks
1 large onion, chopped
2 garlic cloves, minced
2 bay leaves
1 cinnamon stick
8 allspice berries
¼ tsp ground cloves
Finely grated zest of 1 orange
1–2 sprigs of rosemary
200g (7oz) vacuum-packed cooked
  chestnuts
50ml (2fl oz) balsamic vinegar
300ml (10fl oz) Mavrodaphne or other
  sweet red wine
200ml (7fl oz) dry red wine
370g (13oz) tomatoes, peeled and pulsed
  in a blender, or tomato passata (sieved
  tomatoes)
4 tsp tomato purée (paste)
400ml (14fl oz) hot vegetable stock
  or water
Sea salt and freshly ground black pepper

FOR THE CELERIAC PURÉE
850g (1lb 14oz) celeriac (celery root),
  trimmed, peeled and cut into chunks
  (prepared weight)
250g (9oz) potatoes, peeled and cut into
  chunks
1.2 litres (40fl oz) whole milk
1½ tbsp butter
2 tbsp finely grated kefalotyri cheese or
  Parmesan
¼ tsp freshly grated nutmeg
White pepper

continued…

Peel the onions (see Tip below).

Place a large, wide pan over a medium-high heat. Pour in the olive oil and brown the veal cheeks on all sides, cooking two to three pieces at a time to keep the temperature high. Remove the meat to a platter using a slotted spoon and set aside.

Turn the heat down to medium and, in the same pot, sauté the pearl onions, swirling them until they slightly soften and shine, 7–8 minutes. Remove with a slotted spoon and set aside.

In the same pan, sauté the chopped onion until soft and glossy. Add the garlic, bay leaves, cinnamon, allspice, cloves, orange zest and rosemary, season with salt and pepper and stir for about a minute. Stir in the pearl onions and chestnuts and pour in the vinegar and wines. When it starts to simmer, lower the heat to medium-low and return the meat with its juices to the pot, along with the tomatoes and the tomato purée (paste). Add the hot stock or water, season again with salt and pepper if necessary, and as soon as it starts simmering again, cover and bring the heat down to low.

Let it slow-cook for about 1½ hours or until the sauce has thickened and the meat is fork-tender. Keep an eye on it as it cooks and, if it starts to dry out, add a little extra hot stock or water. Adjust the seasoning if necessary and remove from the heat. Let it stand for 15 minutes before serving.

Meanwhile, for the celeriac (celery root) purée, put the celeriac and potatoes in a heavy-based saucepan. Pour in the milk – it should cover them completely. Place over a low heat and gently simmer for 25–35 minutes until soft, stirring occasionally so that they don't stick to the bottom. Remove from the heat and allow to cool for about 10 minutes then, using a slotted spoon, transfer the potatoes and celeriac to a blender (or use a stick blender), reserving any cooking milk. Blend until smooth and creamy, adding a splash of the cooking milk if the purée is too thick, then return to the same pan and place over a very low heat. Stir constantly and mix in the butter and cheese. Season with salt, white pepper and the nutmeg, and remove from the heat.

Serve the *stifado* over the celeriac purée and enjoy.

TIP: PEELING PEARL ONIONS
The onions need to be kept whole and nice-looking after peeling, so be gentle. To peel them with ease, place in a large heatproof bowl and cover with boiling water. Soak for 30 minutes then, using a paring knife, slice off the root end of each onion and carefully squeeze it with two fingers so that the skin pops off.

Karydopita, spiced walnut syrup cake

In Greek mythology, Karya (also spelled Carya) was the daughter of King Dion of Laconia. According to the rather dramatic myth, god Dionysus transformed King Dion's daughter into a tree and that's how the walnut tree got its name; *karya* in ancient Greek, *karydia* in modern Greek.

About 80 per cent of Greece's land surface is classified as mountainous, and is abundant with walnuts: thus, treats are often walnut-centred in these areas. Among the most popular is *karydopita*, or walnut pie, which usually resembles more of a nutty sponge cake. Some recipes around the country use breadcrumbs, while others use flour or semolina, with the most well-known versions from the mountainous regions of Arcadia and Pelion.

This recipe is inspired by the traditional way that it is prepared on mount Pelion, with breadcrumbs and high-quality walnuts, but also adding syrup. The cake pairs really well with ice cream or unsweetened cream, or even yogurt. You can even strain any leftover syrup from the pan and use it on ice cream or yogurt – it's wonderful.

MAKES 18 SQUARES

Oil or butter, for greasing
90g (3¼oz) walnuts, finely ground
80g (3oz) dried breadcrumbs
  (from melba toast or rusks)
1 tsp baking powder
70g (2½oz) caster (superfine) sugar
9 large eggs, separated
½ tsp vanilla extract
50ml (2fl oz) Metaxa or brandy
1 tsp ground cinnamon
½ tsp freshly grated nutmeg
Finely grated zest of 1 small orange
Pinch of salt

FOR THE SYRUP

400g (14oz) caster (superfine) sugar
1 lemon, quartered
2 tbsp lemon juice (can be squeezed
  out of the quartered lemon)

Preheat the oven to 200°C/180°C fan/ 400°F/gas mark 6.

Generously grease the base and sides of a 26cm (10 inch) square cake tin (pan) with oil or butter.

In a small bowl, mix the walnuts, bread-crumbs and baking powder and set aside.

In a stand mixer, whisk the sugar, egg yolks, vanilla and Metaxa (or brandy) together for 2–3 minutes on a medium-high speed until pale and fluffy. Add the cinnamon, nutmeg and orange zest and whisk well.

In a separate bowl, add the pinch of salt to the egg whites and whisk until stiff peaks form. Set aside.

Using a rubber spatula, gradually fold the walnut mixture into the egg yolks until combined. Then, using the rubber spatula, fold in the whisked egg whites. Do not overmix. Pour into the prepared tin (pan) and bake on the middle shelf in the oven for 40–45 minutes until cooked through (check with a knife inserted into the middle; it should come out clean). Remove and let cool for about 1 hour.

The syrup should be poured boiling hot onto the cake, so start preparing it when the cake has already cooled down. Combine all the ingredients with 400ml (14fl oz) water in a small saucepan and bring to a simmer. Gently simmer for about 3 minutes until the sugar dissolves. Gradually pour the syrup over the cake (strain out the lemon quarters), letting each addition absorb before you pour the next. Once you see the syrup staying on the surface, score the cake into portions. I cut it into small squares or diamonds about 4–5cm (1½–2 inches) each side. Cut all the way down to the bottom of the tin. Allow time for the syrup to be absorbed, then serve.

Amygdalota, chewy almond cookies

Almond trees thrive in the Mediterranean, especially the eastern side where they are native. The ancient Egyptians and Persians were particularly fond of them, and Greeks have used them since at least the 6th century BCE.

The symbolism of this nut in Greek culture has for centuries been associated with happiness, prosperity, fertility and good luck. This is why several traditional desserts that are associated with festivities – in particular engagement ceremonies, weddings and baptisms – all feature almonds in one way or another.

Among the most prominent almond treats offered on happy occasions are these *amygdalota*, symbolizing new beginnings.

The basic recipe calls for two main ingredients: finely ground almonds and sugar. Bitter almonds or apricot kernels are often added, in order to add a pleasant aroma and balance the excess sweetness. Egg whites and semolina or breadcrumbs are sometimes added to create a denser texture, while many recipes call for orange blossom or rose water to add a delicate touch of floral aroma and flavour. There are two general categories of Greek *amygdalota*: uncooked, which are softer and more similar to marzipan, and baked, which are my favourite: hard on the outside, moist and chewy on the inside.

The exact recipe, which determines their shape, texture and flavour, always depends on the region or specific island from which they originate. This version is among my favourites.

MAKES ABOUT 30
400g (14oz) blanched almonds
10 bitter almonds or apricot kernels
150g (5oz) granulated sugar
2 large egg whites
Pinch of salt
1½ tbsp orange blossom water

TO FINISH
40ml (1½fl oz) orange blossom water
  (or more, if necessary)
230–250g (8–9oz) icing (confectioners')
  sugar

Preheat the oven to 170°C/150°C fan/340°F/ gas mark 3 (fan setting is best here). Line a large baking tray with baking parchment.

In batches, place the almonds and bitter almonds or apricot kernels in a food processor and grind very finely. Transfer to a bowl and mix in the sugar.

In a separate bowl, whisk the egg whites with the salt to a stiff meringue.

Gradually fold the meringue into the almonds, then add the 1½ tablespoons of orange blossom water and mix until well combined. The mixture should be moist enough to shape.

Shape the mixture into balls, each about 20g (¾oz), then gently press them on the sides to form egg-shaped cookies. Place on the lined tray and bake on a low oven shelf for 20 minutes.

Remove from the oven and let cool completely.

Pour the 40ml (1½fl oz) orange blossom water into a small bowl. Put the icing (confectioners') sugar into a larger bowl or on a plate. Dunk each cookie into the orange blossom water, turning on all sides for a few seconds, then dip into the icing sugar, turning on all sides to coat. Dust off any excess sugar and transfer to the platter to dry. This will form a harder layer on the outside that will keep the interior moist. Repeat with the remaining cookies. Once all the cookies have dried, repeat the coating process for each. Arrange on a platter and serve.

Store in an airtight container.

Variation

To keep them simple and less sweet, skip the coating.

Leave them in a round shape, and before you bake them, gently press a blanched almond into the top of each cookie. When you remove them from the oven and while they are still very hot, spray them with a little orange blossom water and let them cool completely.

Soumada, sweet almond drink

This traditional drink made of almond milk is, like the almond treats on page 172, also offered at happy occasions – particularly engagements and weddings – due to its white colour and the symbolic meaning of almonds. The recipe can be traced to ancient Greece, when it was called 'athasia'; such was the importance of this drink in celebrations, the phrase *stis soumades sou* ('to your *soumades*') was later established as a wish, meaning 'to your happiness' or 'to your wedding'. The drink's sweet flavour is also connected to the concept of happiness, as the wish often goes, 'may your life/wedding be as sweet as this drink.'

Traditionally, it was prepared using a pestle and mortar and required a lot of labour, but now it's common to use a blender. The use of sugar preserves it for longer, but I try to break down the excess sweetness with the use of lemon and bitter almonds. As it can be hard to find bitter almonds, you can use apricot kernels instead; they add a similar bitterness. The orange blossom water adds flavour and aroma, and although it is an optional ingredient, I particularly love it.

It should be served chilled, diluted with water with plenty of ice; during winter it is served warm, like a tea, diluted in hot water and then sprinkled with cinnamon. You can also use it as a syrup to add to cocktails and pastries, and it's particularly good stirred into coffee or tea – hot or iced.

MAKES NEARLY 2 LITRES (4¼ PINTS)
350g (12oz) blanched almonds
30–35 bitter almonds or apricot kernels
600g (1lb 5oz) caster (superfine) sugar
2 strips of pared lemon zest
   (using a swivel peeler)
1 tbsp orange blossom water (optional)
3 tbsp lemon juice, strained

Soak the almonds and bitter almonds (or kernels) overnight in 2.1 litres (60fl oz) water.

The next day, drain the almonds, setting aside 400ml (14fl oz) of the soaking water for the syrup, reserving the rest of the water in a jug (pitcher). Place the almonds in a blender. Pour in enough of the remaining soaking water to just cover the almonds and process well until the almonds are very finely ground. Gradually pour in the remaining water and process. Using a cheesecloth or fine sieve, strain the almond milk, squeezing it hard in order to retrieve as much almond milk as possible. (The almond solids can be used for biscuits and cakes.)

Place the water for the syrup and the sugar in a large saucepan. Add the lemon zest and bring to a gentle boil over a medium-low heat. Simmer for 3–4 minutes until the sugar dissolves. Pour in the almond milk, stir and continue to simmer for about 25–30 minutes over a low heat, stirring occasionally and discarding any foam that forms on the surface, using a slotted spoon. Be prepared to quickly take it off the heat when it rises and remove any foam. It should have a similar consistency to that of a syrup when ready.

Finally, mix in the orange blossom water, if using, and the lemon juice. Remove the lemon zest strips, transfer into sterilized bottles and let cool completely before sealing. It will keep for up to 6 months; I store it in the refrigerator.

Gastrin, ancient Greek *baklava*

———————

The earliest recorded recipe of a predecessor of *baklava* is a Minoan treat called *gastrin*, which derives its name from the ancient Greek word *gastir* (stomach). The recipe is recorded in the 3rd century book *Deipnosophistae*, written by Athenaeus of Naucratis and often referred to as the oldest surviving cookbook. The instructions and description of this dessert are attributed to Chrysippus of Tyana, one of the leading dessert experts of the ancient world.

The ingredients for *gastrin* were the same staples of Greek cuisine that this book focuses on and, at the time, *gastrin* was so nutritious that it was commonly prepared for youngsters as an optimal source of energy. During the Byzantine era, it was still being prepared but called *koptin.* The later versions, renamed *baklava*, were created and developed in the Ottoman palace kitchens.

There are hundreds of regional versions of *baklava* in Greece and in many cases olive oil is used instead of butter.

I believe that the best pastry for this ancient-inspired treat is handmade filo (phyllo), to which I also add sesame seeds. (Store-bought may be also used, brushed with olive oil and sprinkled with the sesame seeds.) I make the filling close to how it is described in the ancient text, but I also add a bit of orange zest, cinnamon and cloves for extra flavour.

Gastrin is free of processed sugar, as the only sweeteners used are honey and grape syrup. It's not too sweet or heavy and can be eaten at all times. As a dessert you can serve it plain or, even better, add a lovely scoop of ice cream on the side.

MAKES 20 SMALL SQUARES

1 quantity of homemade filo (phyllo) pastry (see pages 62–63), with 1 tbsp sesame seeds added to the flour in the first step

Olive oil, for brushing

2 tbsp sesame seeds

FOR THE FILLING

100g (3½oz) ground almonds

100g (3½oz) ground walnuts

40g (1½oz) currants

40g (1½oz) lightly toasted sesame seeds

40g (1½oz) poppy seeds

90g (3¼oz) honey

1 tsp freshly ground black pepper

1 tsp finely grated orange zest

1 tsp ground cinnamon

¼ tsp ground cloves

FOR THE SYRUP

50ml (2fl oz) grape syrup

½ lemon, plus 1 tbsp lemon juice

230g (8oz) honey

Preheat the oven to 220°C/200°C fan/425°F/ gas mark 7 (use non-fan setting if possible).

Divide the filo (phyllo) dough into four equal portions and follow the instructions to roll them out into sheets large enough to fit a rectangular baking tin (pan) that is 21 x 28cm (8 x 11 inches) and 4–5cm (1½–2 inches) deep; bear in mind the pastry sheets will need to be large enough to overhang the edges.

Combine all the filling ingredients in a large bowl. Mix well to combine, using your hands; it should be very sticky (wear gloves). Divide the filling into three equal portions.

Using a brush, grease the base and sides of the baking tin with olive oil. Place the first filo sheet in the centre and gently press it around the base of the tin to fit; the filo should overhang the edges. Evenly sprinkle over the first batch of filling. Place the next filo sheet on top and repeat. Then place the third filo sheet on top and sprinkle with the remaining filling mix. Fold the excess at the edges of the filo layers over the top of the final layer and brush them with olive oil.

Place the final filo sheet on top, brush with olive oil and gently tuck the edges of the filo around the tin to seal.

Using a sharp knife, score portions, cutting right to the base. I cut it into 20 small squares. Sprinkle with the sesame seeds and bake on a low oven shelf for 10 minutes, then reduce the temperature to 190°C/170°C fan/375°F/gas mark 5 and bake for another 50 minutes, until nice and golden. Remove from the oven and let cool completely.

Meanwhile, make the syrup. Combine 150ml (5fl oz) water, the grape syrup, lemon and lemon juice in a small saucepan and bring to the boil. Simmer for about 2 minutes, remove from the heat and let stand for 2–3 minutes to slightly cool before you add the honey. Mix well until it fully dissolves, then pour the syrup over the cooled pie (removing the lemon half) and let it absorb for about 4–5 hours before serving.

Baked feta in filo with a honey-tahini dressing

Feta is made primarily with sheep's milk, often with a small percentage of goat's milk (maximum 30 per cent). It ranges from the very soft, which is creamy and spreadable, to the hard, which is spicier and saltier; the more it ages, the harder it gets. The flavour, which may be milder or stronger, is greatly defined by the region where it is produced, namely the climate and flora of each region, which in turn define the flavour and quality of the milk used in the production. The best feta considered is that which matures in wooden barrels, as this adds an extra spiciness to the cheese.

Feta is a PDO product, strictly produced in specific regions of mainland Greece and on Lesvos island, and all other similar cheeses produced outside of Greece (or even in parts of Greece that are not recognized as official designations of origin) cannot by European law be called feta.

The history of feta goes back to ancient times, as it is believed that the cheese prepared by the Cyclops Polyphemus in Homer's *Odyssey* was in fact the predecessor of what we know today as feta. Through the years, feta has gone by many names: for a long time feta was simply called *tyri*, which means 'cheese', and during the Byzantine era it was named *prosfatos*, which means 'recent', implying its freshness, or *tsantila*, after the cheesecloth used to strain the cheese. The name 'feta', which in Greek means 'slice', was established much later, during the 17th century, deriving from the Italian *fetta* and the Latin *offa, offetta* (mouthful, bite). The reason it was so named is either because of the way it is commonly served (a thick slice on a plate drizzled with olive oil and sprinkled with oregano) or because it is thickly sliced to fit in the barrels or tins filled with brine or buttermilk where it is aged and preserved.

Greeks' 'feta addiction' is unparalleled. This is not just another cheese in Greece (and there are plenty). This is *The* Cheese. Greeks believe it pairs with everything, and in a strange way it does. It is served for breakfast, tops salads, is used in pies and in hundreds of other recipes, and can also be baked, fried or grilled – and I must also mention that charcoal-grilled feta is an absolute dream.

SERVES 4 AS A SHARING PLATE
2 sheets of filo (phyllo) pastry
  (see pages 62–63 for homemade)
Olive oil, for brushing
1 slab of feta, about 180g (6oz), 1.5cm
  (½ inch) thick
½ tsp chilli flakes
1 egg
1–2 tbsp poppy seeds
Pomegranate seeds, to serve

FOR THE SAUCE
3 tbsp honey
1 tsp tahini
1 tbsp lemon juice

Preheat the oven to 210°C/190°C fan/410°F/ gas mark 6½. Line a small baking tray with baking parchment.

Lay the two filo (phyllo) sheets flat on a work surface. Brush one side of the first sheet with olive oil and place the second on top of the first. Place the feta slab in the lower centre of the filo sheets and sprinkle with the chilli flakes (pictured overleaf). Fold the bottom part of the filo on top of the lower part of the feta, tuck the sides in to wrap it well, rolling it all the way up tightly. Seal the edges, using a bit of water to help it stick.

In a small bowl, beat the egg and 1 tablespoon water together. Brush the wrapped feta with the eggwash and sprinkle generously with the poppy seeds. Transfer to the lined tray and bake for 15–20 minutes until golden.

Meanwhile, prepare the sauce. Combine all the ingredients in a bowl with 1 tablespoon water and whisk until smooth. Remove the feta parcel from the oven and transfer to a plate. Drizzle with the sauce and sprinkle with the pomegranate seeds (pictured on page 181). I love to serve it warm while the feta is still melted and creamy, but it can also be served at room temperature.

Note
Instead of baking, you can pan-fry the parcel in a little oil, for about 4 minutes on each side, until golden.

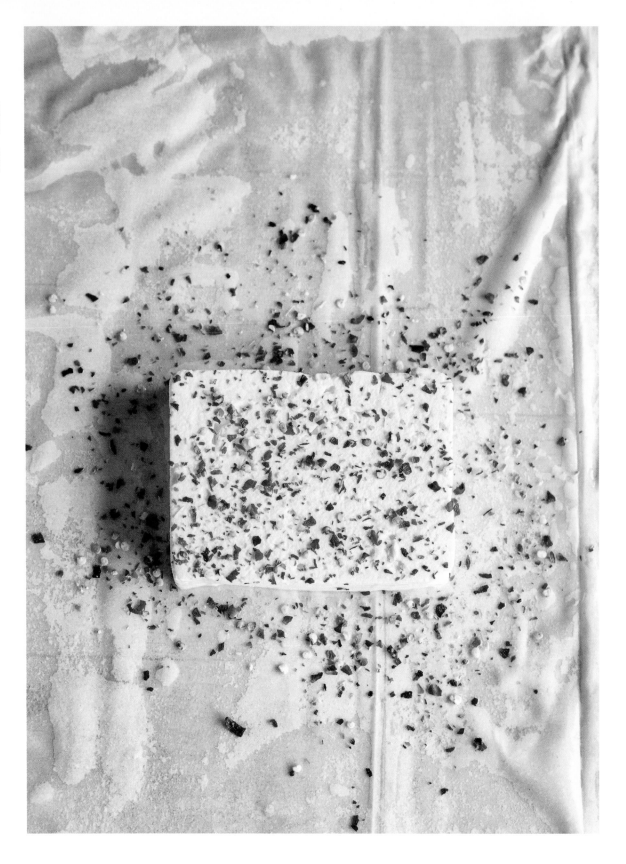

Tahinosoupa, tahini soup with forest mushrooms and leek

Traditional Greek cuisine includes a number of vegan and vegetarian recipes that predominantly focus on seasonal vegetables and pulses. This style of cooking has ancient roots and evolved in the Byzantine era, particularly during the early Christian years when it was also implemented in monasteries and convents. Greeks would traditionally follow long periods of Lent four times a year: Christmas, Easter, The Apostles' (Paul and Peter) fast in June, and on The Assumption of the Virgin Mary in August. In addition to those long Lent periods, which last about 40 days each, the Greek table would also fast weekly, every Wednesday and Friday. Even today there are households that follow this weekly meal planning, sticking to plant-based dishes on those days of the week.

Tahinosoupa is a basic vegan recipe prepared in Greek monasteries, especially on stricter fasting days when even olive oil or wine are prohibited, such as Good Friday. In its most humble version, *tahinosoupa* is very plain, served as a creamy broth with lemon and only a few ingredients. Most versions also add rice, small pasta such as orzo, or *trahanas* (see page 61) to make it more filling. Several monastery versions include mushrooms, usually forest-picked. The soup is delicious and very nutritious and the tahini-lemon combination is often used in contemporary Greek vegan cooking to replace the popular *avgolemono* (egg and lemon sauce).

SERVES 4

280g (10oz) mixed forest mushrooms
2 tbsp olive oil
1 leek, chopped
2 garlic cloves, chopped
1–2 sprigs of thyme
1 tsp dried marjoram
2 tbsp Metaxa or brandy
1.5 litres (56fl oz) hot vegetable stock
  or water
60g (2oz) orzo
60g (2oz) tahini
40ml (1½fl oz) lemon juice
2 tbsp roughly chopped parsley
Sea salt and freshly ground black pepper

Clean the mushrooms with a brush or kitchen paper and roughly chop.

Place a large pan over a medium-high heat. Add the olive oil and sauté the leek for 2–3 minutes until soft. Add the garlic, stir, then mix in the mushrooms, thyme and marjoram. Season with salt and pepper and cook, stirring, for another couple of minutes until most of the liquid has evaporated.

Pour in the Metaxa or brandy, stir and add in the hot stock or water. Cover, lower the heat to medium and simmer for about 30 minutes. Bring the heat up again to a vigorous boil, then add the orzo. Boil for another 7 minutes or until the orzo is cooked to al dente. Remove from the heat, strain off 3–4 ladles of the soup into a jug (pitcher) and set aside.

In a bowl, whisk together the tahini and lemon juice; it will be very thick. Gradually pour enough reserved cooking liquid into the tahini mixture, whisking, until smooth and creamy like a thick sauce. Don't add it too fast or it will turn the mixture lumpy. Pour this into the soup and stir to combine. Serve with black pepper and chopped parsley.

Lagana, sesame-topped flatbread

Lagana is the traditional bread we Greeks make for Clean Monday, the Monday after carnival – 'clean' because this is a day for cleansing: physical, spiritual and literal. Aside from the start of the Easter Lent season, tradition also calls for everyone on this day to wash their pots and pans using hot ash water, and to dye their pavements white.

This crusty flatbread, covered in sesame seeds, is the type of bread that goes hand in hand with *taramosalata* (see picture and recipe on pages 88–89), the popular fish roe dip that is also served that day. Its name derives from the ancient Greek *laganon* or *artolaganon*, a kind of unleavened flatbread prepared with flour and water. References to this type of bread appear in Aristophanes' *Assemblywomen* (391 BCE), and in the works of other ancient writers, including the Roman poet Horace. Athenaeus too, in his 15-volume work *Deipnosophistae*, writes about this flatbread that was kneaded along with wine, some kind of fat (most likely lard) and pepper, then baked over charcoals. Italian focaccia is thought to be a development of these ancient flatbreads (although focaccia is much more oily than Greek *lagana*).

The fact that this bread became associated with Easter is attributed to the Old Testament Jewish tradition of consuming unleavened bread during that period. This, at some point, was altered again and today *lagana* is usually prepared with yeast or sourdough starter.

MAKES 3 LARGE FLATBREADS
25g (1oz) fresh yeast
4 tbsp lukewarm water, plus 300ml (10fl oz)
  for the dough
1 tsp honey
600g (1lb 5oz) strong white bread flour
20g (¾oz) salt
1 tbsp ouzo
Olive oil, for greasing
Sesame and nigella seeds, for sprinkling

In a bowl, dissolve the yeast in the 4 tablespoons of lukewarm water. Mix in the honey and let stand for 10 minutes until frothy.

Put the flour into the bowl of a stand mixer with the dough hook attached. Form a well in the middle and add the yeast mix. Add the salt and start mixing, then pour in the ouzo and slowly start pouring in the 300ml (10fl oz) warm water, mixing on a low speed. Once all the water is incorporated, mix on a medium speed for about 10 minutes. The dough should feel soft and elastic and not too sticky.

Grease a large bowl with olive oil. Shape the dough into a ball and place it in the oiled bowl. Cover and let rise for 30 minutes.

Divide the dough into three equal-sized balls, cover and let rise for another 30 minutes.

Grease three baking trays with olive oil. Take each ball and place it in the centre of a tray. Pour a little olive oil into a small bowl. Dip your fingers in it and start working with the dough, using your fingers and gently opening it up, in a similar way as you would with a focaccia, giving it an oblong shape and indentations. Dip your fingers in the olive oil and gently oil the surface of each flatbread. Sprinkle with sesame and nigella seeds, cover and let rise again for another 30 minutes.

Preheat the oven to 210°C/190°C fan/410°F/gas mark 6½.

Bake for about 30–35 minutes or until golden, swapping the trays around in the oven midway through. Slightly lift it to check it is cooked underneath. For the ultimate crusty exterior, you can spray the breads with water once or twice while they are baking.

VINE

The King of Plants

The vine has for centuries been a prominent and sacred plant that greatly defines the Greek landscape, its gastronomy, and even religion. A symbol of the god Dionysus, it has long been regarded as the 'king' of fruit due to its versatility, highly nutritious profile and medicinal properties. Wine, for example, was one of the most common mortal offerings to thank the gods. Many ancient festivities were devoted to, or revolved around, wine, and it gloriously evolved into enjoying a most prominent place in Greek Christian religion; through its representation of the blood of Jesus, it became a central ingredient in Holy Communion.

It is astonishing how all of the plant can be used (and has been since ancient times) in various and utterly creative ways. Aside from the most common use of the fruit and its plentiful by-products, traditional Greek cuisine pays homage to the vine by using every single part of it, from the tips to the leaves, and even the branches.

Wondrous By-Products

Greek vineyards are some of the richest in the world – they grow all over the country, on the mainland and the islands. There are hundreds of indigenous vine varieties, many of which managed to survive (mostly due to the volcanic, sandy or clay soil) the destructive spread of the minute but devastating bug phylloxera that swept through Europe during the late 19th century.

Vines can be roughly divided into two kinds of grape: those for eating and those used for wine-making, as well as other fermented and distilled products. Those not for eating tend to be smaller in size and have a thicker skin; this gives wine its final flavour and aroma, while also influencing its colour. The process of wine-making itself produces a vast selection of different by-products, such as grape must and molasses, vinegar, *tsipouro* (see page 188) and brandy, including the famous Metaxa (an amber spirit made from Muscat wines, aged wine distillates and Mediterranean botanicals).

The beautiful habit of pairing wine with food is ancient and has long been deeply embedded in Greek culture, regardless of the quality and price of the wine or the drinker's social status. In addition, wine is an absolutely vital ingredient in hundreds of Greek recipes, both savoury and sweet. Just as I choose a particular variety of wine to pair with my food, likewise I select particular varieties of wine for specific culinary purposes. As with all other ingredients, wine adds flavour and aroma to a dish and has the power to really elevate it when used properly; its quality is as important as that of any

other ingredient used. A mere splash of this single ingredient will introduce an irreplaceable note of acid, spice, fruitiness or sweetness and depth. Whereas people have a tendency to add sugar to certain recipes, you can use a sweet wine to achieve the same result. For instance, in a *pastitsio* (see pages 94–95) or *soutzoukakia* (see page 238), I use a sweet red Vinsanto from Santorini or a sweet Mavrodaphne from the Peloponnese to add both sweetness and depth of flavour to the final dish. Likewise, a white and dry, mineral-flavoured Assyrtiko or a citrusy Malagouzia will work perfectly in a seafood or poultry dish, reducing the necessity of too many ingredients in order to achieve fantastic aroma and flavour. A red Agiorgitiko or Xinomavro, combined with the right spices and herbs, will elevate a red meat and dried fruit stew and turn it into a truly festive treat. A sweet white Samos Moschato tastes great in poultry, aside from being enjoyed as a delicious dessert wine; I love to use it in my old-school quince mustard or in light, fruity desserts.

Tsipouro is distilled fragrant grape pomace (skins, seeds and pulp), similar to Italian *grappa*. Containing around 40 per cent alcohol, it is produced from single grape varieties (monovarietal) and its aromas and flavours depend on the grape varieties used. Historically, it has always been an affordable and well liked drink and these days it is increasingly considered a sophisticated option, often used both in cocktails and cooking. Aged versions are also available – usually matured in oak barrels, where the *tsipouro* acquires a deep golden colour similar to brandy. Apart from being among the most popular drinks to accompany meze, it is also traditionally used in the cooking of various dishes, from a lamb roast, to meatballs and biscuits, while the aged variety is typically served as a digestif and pairs outstandingly with dried fruit and bitter chocolate.

Grape must (*moustos*) is the fresh, unfiltered pressed grape juice, before any fermentation process begins. It is high in natural sugars and has been used in Greek cuisine as a primary sweetener since ancient times. You'll find it fresh in farmers' markets, wineries and specialty shops around Greece during wine-making season.

Fresh grape must can also be gently boiled down to become grape molasses, known in Greece as *petimezi*, or grape honey. This natural sweetener is used throughout the year in sweet and savoury dishes. It was primarily used in Greek cuisine before the widespread use of sugar.

Balsamic vinegar is a by-product of concentrated grape must, whereas other vine-derived vinegars are made either directly from fresh grapes or from wine. There are several different kinds of such vinegars in Greece, many of them from single grape varieties, with distinct flavours and aromas, while others are aged or infused with various ingredients like fruit, herbs or spices. Vinegar, like wine, when used right can elevate a recipe – a simple salad of boiled octopus can become an award-winning dish by using the right amount of a good vinegar and a splash of high-quality olive oil. Vinegars are also traditionally used in curing and preserving, marinating fish and seafood, curing pork and even in sausage-making.

Agourida, also known as 'verjus', is the bottled juice of unripe grapes, with a taste somewhere between vinegar and lemon juice. Often used as a replacement for lemons, it is useful in soups and salads, boiled vegetables and even cocktails.

Nature's Best Bounty

Raisins are one of Greece's top exports – until the 20th century, Greece was one of the leading producers of raisins worldwide. Raisins can be made from any variety of grape, and the two leading varieties for drying in Greece are Sultanina (white grape) and the Corinthian currant (small black grape). Both are used in hundreds of recipes, including breads, cakes and puddings, in pies and, of course, in plenty of savoury dishes.

Several written references to the ancient production, commercial use and export of raisins can be found in the works of Homer, Herodotus and Aristotle. Centuries later, raisins were the number one export product of Greece, with production constantly growing. Over time, raisins as a natural sweetener have found many uses, from alcohol production to pastry-making and as a natural sweetener. Since then, former economist and Prime Minister of Greece, Xenophon Zolotas, famously expressed that raisins were to Greece what coffee was to Brazil.

Precious Parcels

The practice of wrapping food in **leaves** is age-old. The ancient Greeks made *thria*, using young, tender fig leaves, which were first blanched and then preserved for use throughout the year in various ways, including wrapping fish or meat, grains or pulses. *Myma* was another similar recipe that resembled what we now know as meatballs and was made with a mix of finely chopped meat or seafood, bulgur and herbs, eaten as is, or wrapped and cooked in vine leaves.

Likewise, today there is still a huge variety of *dolmades* (stuffed leaves) to be found in different regions or islands of Greece throughout the year. *Dolmades* can be simply made with rice or bulgur and chopped herbs, or with a combination of meat. When meat is added they are usually served with a sauce – most typically *avgolemono*.

May is when harvested vine leaves are at their best for *dolmades* – young, tender, light in colour, and delicious. It is also the fresh May harvest that is considered the best for preserving at home, and equally so for buying in jars. The best leaves come from the Sultanina grape variety, abundant in Corinth (south of Athens) and Crete. Vine leaves that are harvested later in the summer (when the leaves are larger and tougher) are still used, but in different ways, such as to wrap and grill a fillet of fish to keep it moist and tender, imparting a hint of its lovely flavour and aroma.

Vine leaves can be dehydrated or even powdered to add a unique flavour and sophisticated touch to a dish or salad. The curly tips of young leaves are harvested during spring and they are mostly pickled or simply boiled for salads and used in seasonal, spring dishes such as my favourite, goat stew with *ambelokorfades* (vine tips).

There are many ways to preserve vine leaves at home. The simplest way is to blanch the leaves for 30–60 seconds, roll about 20 of the leaves up together, tie them with string, close them in an airight freezer bag and store for 8–12 months in the freezer for later use.

Sticks and All

The **branches**, too, add a distinct aroma
to recipes, particularly roasts. Branches
are used mainly in spring, when they are
young, flexible and aromatic. They are
used in traditional vinegar- and sugar-free
pickling, along with a handful of chickpeas
(garbanzos) to help the fermentation
process. Moreover, there are several
traditional Easter roasts that require woven
vine branches to create a natural rack for
the meat to sit on, so that the meat slow-
cooks perfectly and acquires a distinct
aroma. It is also believed that they make
meat more tender.

The vine has long been integral to Greek
cuisine and, over time, has established
a global and timeless identity as a vital
food and drink product. I particularly
love the fact that in both traditional and
contemporary Greek cuisine, we still
use every part of the plant and its by-
products in so many creative and delicious
ways. This kind of holistic use of a single
ingredient shows the utmost respect for
it, and for me this is a great example of
what we should strive for in general in
our cooking and use of produce. I see
this ethos applied more and more in
contemporary cooking and consider it a
very positive step towards the sustainability
that we all wish to achieve for our futures.
Throughout this chapter, my hope is to help
show you how to respect and make use of
everything we have available to us from this
extraordinary plant.

Sougania, stuffed onions from Lesvos with yogurt sauce

This is a dish from Lesvos, an island with a rich history and cuisine. It is the third biggest island in Greece and, due to its large local production, is fairly autonomous. In 1922, the island gave shelter to a large number of Greek refugees who fled Smyrna (present-day Izmir) on the coast of Turkey. Through this, the local cuisine was further enriched, as Greeks from Smyrna were considered legendary cooks and many of them started food-related businesses when they settled in Greece.

I usually make this lovely dish in winter. The onions are often covered with their skins instead of foil while baking; apart from protecting them from burning, the skins add a subtle smoky flavour to the final result which I adore (plus I get to make good use of the skins instead of throwing them away). *Sougania* are most commonly served with their broth as a sauce. Some serve them with *avgolemono,* while I prefer to go for a simple yogurt sauce.

When I make this dish I go for a cut of beef with a higher fat percentage, such as chuck (around 20 per cent), as it adds to the flavour and the texture of the stuffing. You can also replace beef with minced (ground) lamb, if you wish, following exactly the same recipe instructions.

SERVES 6
6 large white onions
1 bay leaf
4 allspice berries
50ml (2fl oz) olive oil
Sea salt and freshly ground black pepper
Chopped parsley, to serve

FOR THE STUFFING
40g (1½oz) medium-grain white rice
2 tbsp olive oil
1 small onion, finely chopped
2 spring onions (scallions), chopped
350g (12oz) minced (ground) beef (ideally chuck/shoulder, see introduction)
1 garlic clove, minced
1 small carrot, grated
1 bay leaf
1 tsp ground cumin
20g (¾oz) currants
20g (¾oz) pine nuts, lightly toasted
50ml (2fl oz) dry white wine
3 tbsp chopped mint
3 tbsp chopped parsley

FOR THE TOMATO SAUCE
1 tbsp olive oil
1 garlic clove, peeled and bashed
1 bay leaf
400g (14oz) tomatoes, grated or chopped
¼ tsp ground cinnamon
1 tbsp tomato purée (paste)
Pinch of sugar (optional; if the tomatoes are too sour)

FOR THE YOGURT SAUCE
250g (9oz) Greek-style (strained) yogurt
25ml (1fl oz) lemon juice
Pinch of ground cumin

For the stuffing, rinse the rice, place in a small bowl and cover with water. Soak for 15–20 minutes, then drain.

Carefully peel the onions and trim the ends, reserving the skins and keeping their shape nice and round. Using a paring knife, make an incision from the top to the bottom of each onion, only cutting halfway through until you hit the core, but no further. The onions need to stay intact, as this will keep the layers whole for peeling and stuffing later. Place the onions in a large pan, cover with water and add a generous amount of salt, the bay leaf and the allspice.

Bring to the boil and simmer for 15–20 minutes until soft and easy to separate into layers. Remove from the heat, drain the onions in a colander and reserve their cooking liquid. With your hands, carefully separate the onion layers, arranging them on a plate ready for use.

For the stuffing, place a large frying pan over a medium-high heat. Add the olive oil and sauté the onion and spring onions (scallions) until soft. Add the minced (ground) meat and brown, stirring, for 2–3 minutes. Mix in the garlic, carrot, bay leaf and rice. Season with salt and pepper, then stir in the cumin. Mix in the currants and pine nuts, then the wine. Bring the heat down to low and gently simmer for a couple of minutes, stirring occasionally. Remove from the heat, discard the bay leaf and mix in the mint and parsley. Taste and adjust the seasoning if necessary.

For the tomato sauce, place a large frying pan over a medium-high heat. Add the olive oil and sauté the garlic clove and bay leaf. Add the tomatoes and cinnamon, mix in the tomato purée (paste) and 150ml (5fl oz)

reserved onion liquid and, if necessary, add in a pinch of sugar. Season with salt and pepper to taste, lower the heat and simmer for 10 minutes until the sauce thickens. Remove from the heat, discard the bay leaf and garlic and adjust the seasoning.

Preheat the oven to 190°C/170°C fan/ 375°F/gas mark 5.

Spoon 3–4 tablespoons of the tomato sauce into a deep baking dish. Use the back of a spoon to spread it over the bottom of the dish. Taking the separated layers of the onions, one at a time, spoon about 1½–2 teaspoons (depending on their size) of stuffing into their centre and wrap the onion 'leaf' around the filling. Place each onion roll in the baking dish, seam side down, arranging them snugly next to each other, touching.

Pour the remaining tomato sauce over the onions, drizzle with the olive oil and pour 3½ tablespoons more of the reserved onion cooking liquid over. Cover the onions with the reserved onion skins (or baking parchment, if you prefer). Seal the whole dish with foil and bake in the oven for 1 hour, then remove just the foil and bake for a further 30–35 minutes.

Meanwhile, prepare the yogurt sauce. I prefer to keep it light and simple here. Reheat another 100ml (3½fl oz) the reserved onion liquid. Place the yogurt in a bowl and mix with the lemon juice and cumin. Slowly pour in the hot onion broth while whisking. You need to do this slowly because the hot liquid will 'shock' the yogurt if poured in too quickly and will ruin the texture of the sauce. Season with salt and pepper to taste.

Serve the onions with the warm yogurt sauce and sprinkled with chopped parsley.

Savoro, pan-fried red mullet with vinegar and currants

Savoro is a simple sauce made with vinegar, garlic and rosemary, prepared on many Greek islands, in parts of the Peloponnese, and in Cyprus. Currants or grape molasses are used to add a subtle sweetness and the final result is a simple, flavourful sauce that works as a preservative as well. Here, interestingly, the marinating process comes after cooking in order to preserve the fried fish for up to two weeks. After the 14th century, this method became popular among fishermen and sailors in particular, who had to be on board for days and therefore find ways of preserving and storing their food on the ship.

It is said that the general idea of this recipe was originally brought to Venice around the 14th century by Sephardic Jews who were involved in trade expeditions throughout the Silk Road, Venice being a central port at the time. Due to being on the road for so long and not being allowed to work or do any kind of physical chores (including cooking) on Saturdays, different methods for preserving food were invented. Often fried small fish – mostly sardines – were placed in vinegar that had previously been gently boiled in order to pickle them. The Venetians altered the recipe and renamed it, enriching it with thinly sliced onions, raisins and pine nuts, adding more flavour. They popularized this version in Constantinople (present-day Istanbul) – with which they had a lot of exchange – and on several Greek islands and in parts of the Peloponnese that were under their occupation. The Greeks in turn added their own twists and slight variations from place to place, and the version here is from Corfu.

Small or medium-sized fish, such as smelt, bogue, picarel and large sardines, are frequently used but the most common – and my personal favourite – variation is with red mullet. Fry the fish whole, with head and bones, as this adds much more flavour to the final result; however, if you are not a big fan of whole fish, you can use fillets.

The fried marinated fish is preserved in the sauce and stored in a container (traditionally a clay container) for up to two weeks. To be honest, *savoro* is so delicious I can never really store it for long and I particularly love eating the fish while still nice and warm with some of the sauce drizzled over it.

SERVES 4
800g (1¾lb) small or medium-sized red mullets (about 7 or 8), scaled and gutted
60g (2oz) plain (all-purpose) flour
300ml (10fl oz) oil, for frying
Sea salt and freshly ground black pepper

FOR THE SAUCE
6 tbsp olive oil
4 large garlic cloves (or 5 smaller), sliced into slivers
1 sprig of rosemary
100g (3½oz) currants
100ml (3½fl oz) white wine vinegar (you can also use red wine vinegar)

Wash the red mullets well. Season with salt, place in a colander and let stand for 15–20 minutes to dry a little.

Spread the flour on a flat platter or tray and coat the mullets, tapping them gently to remove any excess flour.

Place a frying pan over a medium-high heat. Pour in the oil and give it a few minutes to heat up. You can test if the oil is ready by dropping a small piece of bread into it – it will sizzle nicely.

Fry the fish for about 4 minutes on each side until crispy and golden (this will depend a bit on the size of the mullets). Place the fried fish on kitchen paper to drain any excess oil. A general rule when

frying, especially fish, is to not fry too much at once in the same pan, as this will drop the oil temperature and the result will be less crispy, greasier and heavier. I suggest you fry three or four at a time. You may also need to adjust the temperature while you fry after a while, as the oil might get too hot and start burning, browning and overcooking the fish on the outside.

Place a clean pan over a medium heat and add the olive oil for the sauce. Sauté the garlic and rosemary, stirring for a couple of minutes. Add the currants and gently stir for another couple of minutes until they soften a bit. Slowly pour in the vinegar and

lower the heat. Add 6 tablespoons water and season with salt and pepper. Gently simmer for about 10 minutes until the liquid is reduced by a third. Taste the sauce and adjust the seasoning if necessary.

Serve the fish with some sauce drizzled over and store any leftover fish, covered in the sauce, in an airtight container.

Grape 'spoon sweet'

For centuries, preservation was a necessary practice, and for sweet preserves, wine would often be used, with mostly honey or grape molasses (*petimezi*) added as a sweetene. Much later, these would be replaced by sugar when it became more affordable.

'Spoon sweets' are sweet preserves that differ from jam (jelly) and marmalade, mainly in terms of look and texture; the ingredient being preserved should be relatively firm, in good shape, and in a thick, transparent and aromatic syrup. The result should not be too sweet, but balanced with the natural flavours of the main ingredient. They are very contemporary as far as the recent 'zero waste' trend in cooking is concerned. They can be made of: fruit, or just the rind; vegetables, sometimes unripe; flower petals or blossoms; and nuts, when they are unripe, soft rind and shell included. Sometimes a fruit or vegetable preserve might include nuts – usually blanched almonds, added at the end of the process either to stuff the fruit (as with figs and tomatoes) or just mixed in to give it a crunch and an extra kick of flavour (as in the case of pumpkin, quince or grape).

There is indeed a reason why these are called 'spoon' sweets: back in the day, women would welcome guests into their household by presenting an entire jar of homemade preserves, alongside small plates and teaspoons. The guests would use their teaspoon to serve themselves from the jar, placing a spoonful portion on their tiny plate. A glass of fresh cold water is always served alongside the sweet treat, and it is also commonly served with coffee.

Grape 'spoon sweet' offers something very elegant, both in looks and flavour. To start with, grapes are more fragile than other ingredients and it is thus more challenging to keep their shape and firmness; you need good grapes which must be ripe and tasty, yet firm. White grapes tend to be firmer in general, plus they have a golden glow when served with creamy yogurt. However, the same recipe can be made with red. I use the leaves of rose geranium in the syrup which is typically used in several spoon sweet and jam recipes in Greece. I personally love it as it gives a subtle floral taste and aroma. If you have trouble getting it, you can instead use lemon verbena, lemon balm or even basil, or you can just skip it and stick to vanilla. Try your spoon sweet plain or served on yogurt or ice cream as we commonly do in Greece. You can also use it as a topping for cakes or cheesecakes, spooned over panna cotta or other creamy puddings.

MAKES 1 LARGE JAR

1kg (2lb 3oz) green seedless grapes
900g (2lb) caster (superfine) sugar
1 vanilla pod (bean), scored lengthwise
Juice of 1 lemon (2 tbsp)
1–2 rose geranium leaves or 6–7 lemon verbena leaves
60g (2oz) blanched almonds, lightly toasted

Wash the grapes well and let them dry in a colander, then put into a medium saucepan with 280ml (9½fl oz) water, the sugar and vanilla pod (bean). Place over high heat, bring to the boil and cook for 5 minutes. Skim off the froth with a slotted spoon, remove from the heat and set aside to soak overnight.

The next morning, place the pan over a low heat and bring to the boil. Gently simmer for 10 minutes, then remove the grapes from the syrup using a slotted spoon. Transfer to a platter and set aside.

Simmer the syrup for another 10 minutes or so until the syrup is ready. To check, place a saucer in the freezer for 5 minutes. Using a teaspoon, pour a small amount of syrup onto the saucer and spread the

syrup out by moving the saucer in a circular motion. Bringing your mouth close to the saucer, gently blow on the syrup. If small 'waves' form on the surface of the syrup, then it is ready. Add the lemon juice and rose geranium leaves and simmer for another minute, then remove from the heat.

Mix in the toasted almonds and gently add the grapes back into the pan. Let it stand until it cools down, then discard the vanilla and leaves. Store in a sterilized jar, for up to a year. In hot weather, store in the refrigerator.

Fanouropita, a saint's raisin cake

Agios Fanourios (Saint Fanourios) remained unknown until the 14th century, when ruins of an old church were discovered and among the several icons[1] of saints that were found there – most of which were severely damaged – there was just one preserved in good shape. It portrayed a young male saint, dressed in Roman era military apparel, holding a cross with a lit candle fitted on its top. The bishop of Rodos at the time saw the mysterious icon and read out loud the saint's name that was written on it: 'Agios Fano'. The verb *faino* in Greek means 'to shine, and to reveal' and so reflective of the way this lost icon was discovered, the saint became associated with 'lost things' and his name became Fanourios, 'he who reveals'.

In order for him to help you find what you are looking for, whether it's a physical object or simply some good luck, you must first bake a special cake for him.

The number of ingredients used in the recipe is important: it should strictly consist of either seven or nine ingredients in total. Both numbers are symbolic for Christians as they stand for the seven sacred mysteries and the seven days of creation, or the nine orders of angels, and every ingredient has a symbolic connotation.

This cake is vegan, really tasty, and simple to make. It is definitely worth a try, whether you are looking for something lost or not. But in case you are – I hope you find it!

MAKES 40 SMALL PIECES
290ml (9¾fl oz) light olive or sunflower oil, plus extra for greasing
500g (1lb 2oz) self-raising flour
260g (9¼oz) brown sugar
1½ tsp ground cinnamon
¼ tsp ground cloves
1 tsp finely grated orange zest, plus 360ml (13fl oz) juice
1 tsp bicarbonate of soda (baking soda)
160g (5½oz) raisins
50g (2oz) sesame seeds, lightly toasted, plus 2 tbsp to sprinkle on top

Preheat the oven to 180°C/160°C fan/350°F/gas mark 4.

Lightly grease a round 25–27cm (10–10½ inch) cake tin (pan) with oil.

Sift the flour into a medium bowl. To a second, larger bowl, add the oil, sugar, cinnamon, cloves and orange zest and mix well, using a whisk, until it turns thick and almost creamy.

Pour the orange juice into a large glass. Add half the juice to the oil mixture and whisk for about a minute. Holding the glass with the rest of the orange juice over the mixing bowl, add the bicarbonate of soda (baking soda) and stir. The bicarbonate of soda will rise and froth; mix it all into the wet ingredients. Add the raisins and sesame seeds and gently fold, while gradually adding in the flour as well. Once all the flour is incorporated, the cake mix should look slightly runny. Pour it into the greased cake tin and sprinkle with the 2 tablespoons of sesame seeds. Bake for 50–55 minutes, or until a skewer inserted into the middle comes out clean. Remove from the oven and let cool before removing it from the cake tin.

---

[1] Religious painting of a saint.

Moustalevria, grape must pudding

In Greece, September is also called *trygitis* (grape harvest). Beginning around mid-August, depending on the region, it takes place mostly throughout September (especially for the wine-making grape varieties). That is when a brownish-coloured, jelly-like pudding, known as *moustalevria*, makes its annual appearance in shops and markets.

Must is a very seasonal ingredient as it needs to be fresh and doesn't last more than 2–3 days in the refrigerator. This is why it is stored in the freezer for future use throughout the year. You can buy bottles of pure grape must in farmers' markets or specialty shops around Greece when in season.

Moustalevria, made for centuries, is essentially a pudding made entirely out of grape must, set with the addition of flour and served sprinkled with cinnamon and ground nuts or sesame seeds. If you can't get hold of grape must, you can use grape molasses instead. Or, even better, make your own fresh grape must (even with grapes that are not meant for wine-making). I advise you not to use a juicer or blender; use your hands instead to squeeze them over a sieve and then strain it through a cheesecloth.

The traditional way yields the the best results and a good shine. You first need to 'clean' it, by boiling it with wood ash (enclosed in a sachet) or a slice of bread. Only after this process is the grape must ready for use. (See page 205 for directions for this preparation.)

SERVES 6–8
80g (3oz) ground walnuts
2 tbsp toasted sesame seeds
1 tbsp ground cinnamon, plus extra for
  sprinkling
1 litre (34fl oz) prepared grape must
  (see Note overleaf)
130g (4½oz) plain (all-purpose) flour, sifted
2–3 tbsp chilled water

In a small bowl, mix the ground walnuts with the sesame seeds and cinnamon and set aside.

Add 500ml (17fl oz) of the grape must to a bowl and gradually stir in the flour, using a whisk, until the mixture looks nice and smooth (we don't want any lumps). Slowly mix in the rest of the grape must and finally pass it through a fine sieve into a large saucepan. Gently bring to the boil and simmer, stirring constantly with a whisk, until it has a creamy and velvety consistency (similar to that of a custard), no longer than 5–7 minutes. Remove from the heat and mix in the chilled water.

Divide it into individual bowls or glasses and let it cool down for 10 minutes. Place it in the refrigerator to set and sprinkle with extra cinnamon and the ground nuts and seeds before serving.

continued…

Note

To make grape must from scratch, start the process in the evening as it requires about 12 hours of resting. Wash the grapes, remove the stems and, using your hands, press them over a sieve. Strain through a cheesecloth. Place the juice in a large pan. For every 2 litres (70fl oz) of juice, add 2 tablespoons of wood ash or 1 regular slice of stale bread. Bring the juice to the boil and lower the heat to a simmer; it will start to froth and you need to skim off this froth using a slotted spoon. Remove from the heat when it stops frothing. Cover with a clean dish towel and let it stand overnight. The next morning, strain it well through the cheesecloth until the liquid looks clean and clear (when you do this cleansing process with bread, the colour of the grape must will be paler compared to using the ash). Transfer to clean bottles and store in the refrigerator for a day, or freezer for up to a year (or you can use it immediately for the recipe).

Sykomaida, traditional dried fig 'salami'

There are several slight variations of this recipe, prepared in different parts of Greece, but Corfu's is especially famous. Even though Corfu does not belong to the 'big fig' regions, such as Kalamata in the Peloponnese or Kymi on Euboea Island, the version made there is by far the most popular in Greece (pictured on page 211). What makes it special is the bountiful, pleasantly spicy use of ground black pepper. Ideally the figs should be sun-dried (as tradition calls for in Greece), then the fig paste is kneaded with grape juice, grape must or grape syrup (molasses), nuts or dried fruit, orange zest, fennel seeds and often a splash of ouzo. Usually they give it a round, flat patty-like shape, but on Corfu they also give it a small cylinder (salami) shape and roll it in sesame seeds, which is also divine. After the *sykomaida* is dried (either sun-dried as tradition calls or oven-dried), it is wrapped in fresh leaves such as vine, chestnut tree or fig leaves and can be preserved for a whole year. Alternatively, you can just stick it on a couple of bay leaves (they preserve it) and wrap it in clingfilm (plastic wrap).

To serve, slice it thinly and pair it with cheese or cold cuts, or you can even serve it plain and paired with a glass of *tsipouro* or ouzo, as is the custom in Greece. Another way I love to use it is in salads or sandwiches; try it in a sandwich with a creamy white cheese or with warm Camembert and some watercress or rocket (arugula). I also serve it after dinner with dessert wine and aged cheese.

MAKES 4 PIECES

500g (1lb 2oz) dried figs

150ml (5fl oz) unsweetened grape juice (ideally fresh, from 230g/8oz fresh seedless grapes, see method)

50ml (2fl oz) ouzo

2 tsp black peppercorns

2 tsp fennel seeds

60g (2oz) blanched almonds, lightly toasted, then roughly chopped

Pinch of sea salt

Finely grated zest of 1 medium orange

1 tsp thyme leaves

¼ tsp ground cloves

Sesame seeds, to coat (optional)

Chop the figs and place them in a medium-sized bowl.

I like sticking to the traditional way and use fresh grapes as ready-made juices tend to be sweeter. Wash the grapes thoroughly and let them drain in a colander. Squeeze them with your hands to get their juice out or simply place them in a blender and juice them. Strain the juice through a fine sieve. Add the juice and ouzo to the chopped figs and mix. Cover and let stand for 2 hours to soften.

Place 3–4 tablespoons of figs in a food processor and pulse to a paste. Keep adding more of the figs to the processor until they are all used up.

Crush the peppercorns and fennel seeds with a pestle and mortar. (You can use a food processor but make sure they stay coarsely ground.)

Add the chopped almonds, salt, orange zest, thyme leaves, cloves, and crushed peppercorns and fennel seeds to the fig paste. Cover with a cloth and let stand overnight.

The next morning, divide the paste into four equal parts. Shape them as you prefer, either into four small salamis or patties.

Traditional methods dry them in the sun for about a week. If you choose to do that, it's best you brush them with a bit of extra ouzo and cover them with something light like a piece of tulle, to protect them from insects.

Drying them in the oven is faster and easier, especially for those of you not living on a Greek island. Line a baking tray with baking parchment and place the shaped fig patties on it.

Turn on the oven at 50°C/120°F/gas lowest, place the tray on the middle shelf and leave for 2½–3 hours until they feel dry. Allow to cool completely.

If you wish to coat them in sesame seeds (either lightly toasted or raw), cover the surface of a plate with the seeds and roll the shaped fig paste on it until evenly coated.

Wrap in leaves (see pictures overleaf) or clingfilm (plastic wrap) and store in an airtight container along with a few bay leaves to preserve them in good shape for up to a year.

PLANT

Pickled vine fronds

I love the little curly fronds that grow on vines in spring. Several seasonal recipes include the fresh fronds, from lamb and goat stews, to vegetarian rice or pulse dishes and, of course, salads. Due to their short season, it is common to pickle them. You can buy them fresh at farmers' markets around Greece during May, while many people, like my mother, prefer to pick them themselves straight from the blooming vines. Small, young leaves are left on the curly sprigs.

The pickled fronds are used in various ways, in a similar way to capers or pickled rock samphire, or to garnish a variety of different meze dishes. I love adding them to fancy platters with cold cuts or cheese and they can also be included in sandwiches or in various types of salad, including a classic Greek or a potato salad. The process here is simple, as with most kinds of pickle, but it is important that the fronds are fresh and tender.

MAKES 1 LARGE JAR
500g (1lb 2oz) freshly picked, tender vine fronds
25g (1oz) natural sea salt
2 bay leaves
270ml (9½fl oz) white wine vinegar
1 tsp black peppercorns
1 tsp pink peppercorns
1 tsp coriander seeds
3–4 small garlic cloves, peeled
130ml (4½fl oz) olive oil

Wash the fronds and set aside to dry in a colander. Bring a large pan of water to the boil. Add ½ tablespoon of the salt and turn off the heat. Submerge the vine fronds with the bay leaves in the boiling water and leave for 5–10 minutes until their colour slightly changes. I like to keep them a bit firm and crispy, and the longer you leave them in the hot water, the softer they will get.

Drain, rinse in cold water (a bowl of iced water would be ideal) and allow to drain and cool down to room temperature. Reserve the blanched bay leaves.

In a large jug (pitcher) mix 250ml (9fl oz) measured water with the remaining salt until it dissolves. Mix in the vinegar and set aside.

Mix the black and pink peppercorns and coriander seeds in a small bowl and set aside.

Place a third of the vine fronds on the bottom of a large sterilized jar that has a lid. Add half the mixed spices, 1 bay leaf, and 1–2 garlic cloves. Place another third of the fronds on top and add the remaining spices, bay leaf and garlic. Place the rest of the fronds on top, pour in the vinegar-water mix and finally top it up with the olive oil. The liquid in the jar should cover the fronds completely. If it doesn't, add a little more vinegar or olive oil.

Cover and store in a cool, dry place for 20–30 days before opening. Once opened, store in the refrigerator.

Stuffed sardines wrapped in vine leaves with olive oil and lemon sauce

Sardines, widely consumed by Greeks since ancient times, are among the most nutritious fish, packed with omega-3 fatty acids, vitamins D and B12, calcium and other important minerals. They are abundant in the Mediterranean, very affordable and, due to the fact that they are small and eat only plankton, their mercury content is very low. There are hundreds of wonderful traditional Greek recipes that use sardines in the most simple, creative ways.

Lesvos, the island of ouzo, is equally famous for sardines, primarily those fished in the Gulf of Kalloni; also known as *papalines*, they are said to be the best in the whole of Greece. They are pale and not very large, but they do get chubby. What they are mostly famous for is their fine flavour, which is due to the microclimate and the nutrients that, through rivers and streams, flow into the Gulf of Kalloni.

Sardines are fished between early July and October, with over 100 tons of this local variety fished annually. The best month to fish them is August, when the three-day Sardine Festival takes place. Like in all traditional festivals held in Greece, there's live music and dancing and cooking involved, with grilled sardines offered to visitors alongside glasses full of ouzo.

The idea of wrapping fish in leaves comes from the ancient Greeks. It can be done with any type of fish, from small ones like sardines to a large whole fish or even fillets, such as tuna, swordfish or salmon. The leaf protects the fish from burning and keeps it moist, while the unique flavour of vine leaves adds to the taste and appealing presentation.

SERVES 4

30–40 vine leaves (depending on the number of sardines), fresh (ideally) or from a jar

180g (6oz) teardrop or cherry tomatoes, diced

500g (1lb 2oz) fresh or frozen sardines, scaled and butterflied (ask your fishmonger to do this or see TIP opposite)

1 tbsp capers (rinsed if salt-packed), chopped

4 garlic cloves, minced

3 tbsp chopped parsley

1 tsp dried oregano

50ml (2fl oz) olive oil

40ml (1½fl oz) lemon juice

Sea salt and freshly ground black pepper

FOR THE DRESSING

1½ tbsp lemon juice

¼ tsp mustard powder

40ml (1½fl oz) extra virgin olive oil

2 tsp chopped parsley

Bring a large pan of water to the boil over a medium-high heat. Blanch the vine leaves a few at a time for about 3 minutes. Remove with a slotted spoon and place them in a bowl with chilled water and ice. To drain, carefully hang them over the sides of a colander and leave to dry for 20 minutes or so.

Place the diced tomatoes in a colander and let them sit for 15 minutes to drain.

Season the sardines with salt and pepper.

In a medium bowl, combine the tomatoes, capers, garlic, parsley, oregano, salt and pepper to taste, and 1 tablespoon of the olive oil. Mix and set aside.

Preheat the oven to 200°C/180°C fan/ 400°F/gas mark 6.

Place a vine leaf on the work surface, vein side up. Trim the stem if it's sticking out from the bottom. Place a butterflied sardine in the middle. Add about 1 teaspoon of the filling mixture to the sardine, fold it and wrap it in the leaf, tucking in the two ends as you fold, like a small burrito. Repeat with the rest of the sardines and filling.

Drizzle 1 tablespoon of olive oil into the base of a baking dish, measuring 30 x 22cm (12 x 8½ inches). Arrange the wrapped sardines, seam side down, in the dish, side by side. Season with salt and pepper and drizzle over the lemon juice and remaining olive oil. Bake on the middle shelf of the oven for about 30 minutes until the leaves are slightly charred.

Meanwhile, make the dressing. Mix the lemon juice with the mustard powder in a small bowl until it dissolves. Slowly pour in the olive oil, while whisking. The dressing should turn pale and thick. Season with salt and pepper and mix in the chopped parsley.

Remove the dish from the oven and use a slotted spoon to transfer the wrapped sardines to a platter (leaving the liquid in the baking dish). Drizzle with the dressing and serve.

TIP: SCALING SARDINES

Run a fish scaler or blunt knife along the fish from the tail towards the head to remove any loose scales, then wash thoroughly in a sink of cold water. Using kitchen scissors or a paring knife, gently cut around the head and pull it off, removing it with the entrails. Cut along the stomach and open it up, then grab the spine and gently pull it out.

Vine leaf yogurt and cheese pie

Traditionally, this time-saving method is used to make regular *dolmades* or *dolmadopites* (dolma pies) filled with rice or bulgur mixed with lots of herbs – with or without minced meat. On Lesvos and in Drama, a great wine region in the north, they make vine leaf pies filled with yogurt and/or cheese, and most of the traditional recipes that I have come across are prepared with sheep's milk yogurt. I love including feta in this pie and I also add *anthotyro*, a fresh, mild, creamy, white cheese very similar to ricotta. The herbs, as usual, have an important impact on the flavour and success of the pie (pictured on page 219).

Fresh vine leaves can be hard to find in some parts of the world, and the jarred ones work just fine here, as long as they are of good quality. Ideally, choose those stored in glass jars and go for the paler green leaves. The darker and shinier the leaves, the tougher they tend to be and, often, there is a stronger flavour from the brine. In any case, the thicker the leaves, the longer they need blanching. You could also substitute fresh vine leaves with leaves such as kale (remove the central stem of the kale) or, even better, chard.

SERVES 6

About 40 vine leaves, fresh or from a jar
200g (7oz) feta
200g (7oz) *anthotyro* cheese, or ricotta
250g (9oz) Greek-style (strained) yogurt
½ tsp ground coriander
3 tbsp chopped mint leaves
2 tbsp chopped dill
½ tsp finely grated lemon zest
2 spring onions (scallions), including the
 green part, chopped
Olive oil, for brushing and drizzling
Sea salt and freshly ground black pepper

TO SERVE

2 tomatoes, deseeded, diced and drained
1 tsp chopped mint
2 tsp chopped spring onion (scallion),
 optional
4–5 tbsp Greek-style (strained) yogurt
Smoked sweet paprika

Bring a large pan of water to the boil over a medium-high heat. Blanch the vine leaves, a few at a time, for about 3 minutes (depending on the quality of the leaves). Remove with a slotted spoon and place them in a bowl with chilled water and ice. To drain, carefully hang them over the sides of a colander and leave to dry for about 20 minutes or so.

Crumble the feta into a large bowl, using your hands or a fork. Mix in the *anthotyro* (or ricotta) and yogurt until evenly combined. Add the ground coriander seeds, herbs, lemon zest, spring onions (scallions), and some black pepper to taste. Mix well and set aside.

Preheat the oven to 200°C/180°C fan/ 400°F/gas mark 6.

Brush the base and sides of a round, shallow baking tin (pan), 25cm (10 inches) in diameter, with a little olive oil. Start layering the leaves, beginning from the sides of the pan, laying them one next to the other and slightly overlapping. The top half of the leaves should be hanging over the rim of the tin (they will be folded over the filling), and the base and sides covered (using about 15 of the leaves). Brush with olive oil then create a second layer of leaves in exactly the same manner, covering both the base and side of the pan, making sure there are no little gaps between the leaves. Gently pat dry with some kitchen paper, then spoon in the filling, spreading it evenly with the back of a tablespoon. Fold in the overhanging leaves and layer the remaining

continued…

leaves on top. Brush with a little olive oil and make sure it is sealed, without any gaps. Tuck the leaves around the edges down into the tin using a knife, to ensure it is fully sealed and smooth all the way around, then brush the final layer with olive oil.

Place a piece of baking parchment on top of the pie, gently pressing it down to stick to the leaves. Spray with a little water then cover the whole thing with foil.

Bake on the lowest shelf in the oven for 35 minutes, then remove the foil and baking parchment and bake for another 10–15 minutes. Remove and allow to cool a little (you can serve it either warm or cold).

Mix the tomatoes with the mint, spring onions (scallions) and a little salt. Spoon the yogurt over the top of the pie, creating a thin, even layer. Create another layer with the diced tomato mix on top.

Slice the pie like a pizza and serve it drizzled with a few drops of olive oil and sprinkled with a little smoked paprika.

Beef *dolmades* with *avgolemono* sauce

I believe that everyone has certain dishes that, one way or another, are inextricably linked with memories of certain people. In my case, beef *dolmades* in luscious *avgolemono* sauce is something I connect to my grandmother, Rena, who influenced my love of this dish, and I think of her every single time I make or eat it. Her husband, my grandfather George, a grand lemon lover, really became an expert in *avgolemono* sauce. I have vivid memories of him standing over a bowl with the frothy egg sauce, beating with a whisk, while my grandmother gently poured in warm broth from the pot.

Dolmades are prepared all over Greece with different kinds of leaves or fillings. During winter, cabbage is commonly used, and stuffed cabbage rolls with pork is one of the traditional dishes prepared in Greece on Christmas day. This custom is rooted in Byzantine practices and Greek Orthodox religion, and the cabbage leaves wrapped around the filling stand for the swaddling clothes that baby Jesus was wrapped in.

Serve with fresh bread.

SERVES 6–8

70–80 vine leaves, fresh or from a jar
500g (1lb 2oz) minced (ground) beef
  (or half pork, half beef)
1 medium onion, chopped
3 spring onions (scallions), including the
  green part, chopped
2 tbsp chopped parsley (reserve the stems)
2 tbsp chopped mint (reserve the stems)
2 tbsp chopped dill (reserve the stems)
160ml (5½fl oz) olive oil
90g (3¼oz) short-grain white rice
1 tsp salt
2 tbsp lemon juice
Hot vegetable stock or water
Freshly ground black pepper

FOR THE *AVGOLEMONO* SAUCE
2 large eggs
80ml (3fl oz) lemon juice (or more or less,
  to taste)
2 tsp cornflour (cornstarch)

Bring a large pan of water to the boil over a medium-high heat. Blanch the vine leaves a few at a time for about 3 minutes (depending on the quality of the leaves). Remove with a slotted spoon and place them in a bowl with chilled water and ice. To drain, carefully hang them over the sides of a colander and leave to dry for 20 minutes or so.

Put the minced (ground) meat in a bowl and add the onion, spring onions (scallions), herbs, half the olive oil, the rice, and salt and black pepper to taste. Knead well to combine.

Lay the reserved herb stems on the base of a large, heavy-based pan. On top lay any small or torn vine leaves – one layer is enough.

Start rolling: place a leaf on the work surface, vein side up. Trim the stem if it's sticking out from the bottom. Add about 1 full teaspoon of the filling mixture to the lower centre part of the leaf. Fold the left side of the leaf to the centre, on top of the meat filling, then fold the right side on top, then start rolling from the bottom to the top (like a spring roll). Repeat with the remaining leaves and filling.

Place the stuffed leaves seam side down in the pan, in a spiral shape, adding more layers, also in a spiral shape. When all the leaves are filled and are nicely laid in the pan, drizzle over the remaining olive oil and the lemon juice. Place a plate upside down on top of the stuffed vine leaves in the centre of the pot. Pour in enough warm stock or water to cover the plate (the weight from the plate will prevent them from opening and preserve their nice shape). Cover and bring to a simmer over a medium-high heat. When it starts simmering, bring the heat down to medium and simmer for 20 minutes, then lower the heat further and gently simmer for another 20 minutes. (Total cooking time should be about 40 minutes.)

Remove the lid and, pushing the plate gently down with a spoon (the plate will be burning hot), carefully pour the warm liquid from the pan into a jug (pitcher) or bowl. Use a spoon to remove the plate. Set aside.

The way to make *avgolemono* sauce differs slightly depending on the dish you are cooking. If you are planning to reheat this later, I recommend you add the cornflour (cornstarch) and follow the directions here. If you are planning to finish it all in one go, then you can skip the cornflour, just add the lemon juice straight to the eggs and you won't need to thicken it up on the stovetop; instead, after you fold it with the egg whites and mix it with the hot liquid, just pour it into the *dolmades*.

Separate the eggs. Beat the whites to soft peaks (a light meringue, not too stiff).

In a small bowl, mix the lemon juice with the cornflour. Beat the egg yolks well, then add the lemon juice mixture to the yolks and beat. Fold in the whites and transfer to a small saucepan. Place over a low heat and start adding the warm *dolmades* cooking liquid very slowly, whisking constantly. When it feels nice and thick, take it off the heat and pour it into the *dolmades*. Place the lid on the pot, secure it by holding it with both hands, and shake well. This method (rather than stirring with a spoon) keeps your *dolmades* from becoming mushy. Serve with ground black pepper.

Spinach and feta stuffed chicken rolls wrapped in vine leaves

This filling is similar to the one I prepare for a spinach pie. I add a bit of feta for flavour and texture, and also because feta and fresh herbs are a great match with the vine leaves. The stuffed chicken breasts are then rolled in vine leaves, which keep them nice and moist, and add their unique aroma to the chicken. This is a light, tasty dish that can be served warm as a main with a simple side like rice, potatoes or salad. You can also let the rolls cool completely and then slice them into thinner rounds to serve cold as a meze dish or a starter with a bit of yogurt on the side.

SERVES 4-6

4 large boneless chicken breasts (around 350g/12oz each)
2 tbsp olive oil
1 tbsp lemon juice
½ tsp ground cumin
48 vine leaves (fresh or from a jar)
Sea salt and freshly ground black pepper

FOR THE STUFFING

2 tbsp olive oil
1 leek, including the green part, chopped
4 spring onions (scallions), including the green part, chopped
1 red (bell) pepper, diced
1 garlic clove, chopped
180g (6oz) spinach leaves, trimmed and roughly chopped
2 tbsp chopped dill
1 tbsp chopped mint
½ tsp finely grated lemon zest
50g (2oz) feta, crumbled
Sea salt and freshly ground black pepper

Place the chicken breasts on a platter and drizzle them with the olive oil and lemon juice. Season with the cumin and some salt and black pepper, and gently rub them on both sides. Cover with clingfilm (plastic wrap) and marinate in the refrigerator for 15–30 minutes.

Place each chicken breast between two pieces of clingfilm and, with a meat mallet (or a heavy rolling pin), bash out the pieces until they are about 5mm (¼ inch) thick, then remove the clingfilm.

Bring a large pan of water to the boil over a medium-high heat. Blanch the vine leaves a few at a time for about 3 minutes (depending on the quality of the leaves). Remove with a slotted spoon and place them in a bowl with chilled water and ice. To drain, carefully hang them over the sides of a colander and leave to dry for 20 minutes or so.

Place a large, deep pan over a medium-high heat. Pour in the olive oil and, once hot, sauté the leek until starting to soften. Add the spring onions (scallions), red (bell) pepper and garlic and stir for another couple of minutes. Add the spinach in batches, gently tossing it until wilted. Season with salt and pepper, then remove from the heat and mix in the dill, mint and lemon zest. Transfer to a colander (or sieve if your colander still has vine leaves drying) and let it drain for 10–15 minutes. Transfer to a bowl and mix in the crumbled feta. Adjust the seasoning if necessary.

Preheat the oven to 210°C/190°C fan/ 410°F/gas mark 6½.

Cut out 4 pieces of baking parchment, each large enough to fit a chicken breast (about 30 x 35cm/12 x 14 inches). Cover the surface of each parchment with vine leaves, laying them out side by side and overlapping so that they cover around half of the neighbouring leaf, creating two layers on each (about 12 leaves in total on each parchment).

Place a chicken breast on top of each vine leaf layer and spoon about 2–3 tablespoons

of the spinach mixture across the middle, keeping the top side free to be able to seal it well once rolled. Gently grab it from the bottom side of the leaves and start rolling it tightly like a sushi roll, ensuring the leaves are wrapping the whole roll. Once the roll is shaped, grab the parchment paper and roll it all up, sealing the ends well by twisting the paper like a sweet (candy) wrapper. Place the rolls in a baking dish, side by side, and bake in the oven for 45–50 minutes (check one by unwrapping to see if it is done).

Remove from the oven and leave wrapped for 5–10 minutes, then remove the parchment and slice each into rounds, about 2cm (¾ inch) thick.

Mastelo, Easter lamb baked over vine twigs

This is a typical Easter dish from Sifnos, one of the Cycladic Islands. Sifnos is known for its ceramics (a lot of which are used for cooking) and its truly wonderful local cuisine. The name of this dish derives from a special type of ceramic pot (*mastelo*) that is made on Sifnos; it has a slightly conical shape, resembling a large flower pot or bucket, with a narrow base and a wide opening on top. Unlike other local ceramic pots that were initially meant to be used in wood-burning ovens, this one does not have a fitted lid. All kinds of ceramic pots were originally made to be used in wood-burning ovens, but these days are also used in conventional ovens.

For this ancient recipe, vine twigs placed on the base of the pot serve as a rack, while adding flavour to the dish. Using vine twigs for roasts during spring when the twigs are young, flexible and fragrant is a habit also found in other parts of Greece. Typically, the meat would be lamb, goat and pork, or a combination of lamb and goat, as is often the case on Sifnos.

The secret to this recipe is the long, slow roasting of the meat in red wine, which is aromatized with dill. This is a really great method for braising meat, whether or not you have the right ceramic pot – you can use any ovenproof ceramic dish, lidded casserole dish or another deep baking dish. Tradition says that this meat can be preserved outside the refrigerator for 40 days, but to be honest it always disappears on the day I cook it.

SERVES 6

3–4 vine twigs (young and flexible)
2kg (4lb 6oz) lamb (or goat, or half-and-half) on the bone, cut into pieces about 200g (7oz)
1 bottle of dry red wine
9–10 tbsp chopped dill
Sea salt and freshly ground black pepper

Bend and fit the vine twigs on the bottom of an ovenproof ceramic pot or pan, crosswise, to form a natural rack.

Wash the meat in cold running water. Locals first wash it with water and then with red wine, but I hate wasting the wine, so instead I wash it with water and then I marinate it in the red wine.

Place the meat in a container, ideally glass, pour over the wine, cover with clingfilm (plastic wrap) and marinate in the refrigerator overnight or for about 8 hours.

The next day, drain the meat, reserving 250ml (9fl oz) of the wine.

Preheat the oven to 220°C/200°C fan/425°F/gas mark 7.

Pat the meat dry with kitchen paper and season generously with salt and pepper. Place some of the pieces of meat in a single layer on top of the vine twig rack. Sprinkle with some chopped dill, then create a second layer of meat on top and sprinkle with dill again. Repeat until all the meat and dill are used. Finally, pour in the reserved wine. If you don't have a lid for your pot or dish, cover it with baking parchment, tying it tightly around the pot or baking dish using kitchen string. Add a sheet of foil on top.

Bake in the oven for 40 minutes, then lower the heat to 160°C/140°C fan/320°F/gas mark 2½ and bake for another 2–2½ hours until the liquid in the pan is absorbed and the meat is tender enough to fall off the bone. If baking in a wood-burning oven, bake for 4–5 hours.

Goat fricassée with vine leaves and greens

This dish is a celebration of spring and a great example of how traditional Greek cooking uses meat, which is more about adding flavour to a dish than actually consuming a large amount of protein; although this dish relies on the vegetables. Fricassée is a kind of stew usually prepared with green leaves – it can be wild edible weeds that grow locally every season, such as nettles or leaves, or chard, lettuce, spinach or vine leaves, along with plenty of chopped onions and herbs. Variations use other spring vegetables, such as artichokes. Although the name fricassée is borrowed from French cuisine (pieces of meat browned in butter, then cooked in stock and served in a white sauce with cream or milk and butter), the Greek take is quite different.

Greek fricassée is most commonly prepared with lamb, goat, pork, rabbit or chicken. Other glorious versions of this recipe use mushrooms, field snails or fish, but my personal favourite is with goat or lamb. When the dish is ready, we prepare an egg and lemon sauce with its broth. The lemon really brings out the freshness and amazing flavours of this dish, which is really a cross between a stew and a soup. To properly enjoy it, serve it in a slightly deep plate with lots of broth (almost like a soup) and fresh crusty bread to dunk in it. This recipe is among my most favourite comforting and nutritious dishes, and I do urge you to make it if you are a lover of greens, lemons and herbs, as I am.

I find it essential to use meat on the bone as it will make your dish far tastier and messier to eat, which is always a good thing!

SERVES 4

220g (7¾oz) vine leaves, fresh or from a jar
1.5kg (3lb 5oz) goat shoulder (or lamb shoulder) on the bone, cut into smaller pieces of about 100–130g/3½–4½oz) – ask your butcher to do this for you
50ml (2fl oz) olive oil
1 onion, chopped
1 leek, including the green part, chopped
5–6 spring onions (scallions), including the green part, roughly chopped
1 garlic clove, quartered
100ml (3½fl oz) dry white wine
1 litre (34fl oz) warm vegetable stock
380g (13½oz) chard, trimmed and roughly chopped
250g (9oz) lettuce, roughly chopped
8 tbsp roughly chopped dill
5 tbsp mint leaves, roughly chopped
1 tsp cornflour (cornstarch)
80ml (3fl oz) lemon juice (about 1 lemon)
2 eggs
Sea salt and freshly ground black pepper

If using vine leaves from a jar, drain and rinse them.

Fill a medium cooking pot halfway up with water and place over a medium-high heat. When the water starts to boil, lower the heat to medium-low and add the vine leaves. Gently simmer for 7–8 minutes (if you are using fresh leaves, 3–4 minutes should be enough). Drain, roughly chop and set aside.

Season the goat with salt and pepper.

Place a wide, deep pan over a medium-high heat and add the olive oil. Once hot, add the goat pieces and gently brown on all sides. Remove the goat from the pan, place on a plate and set aside.

Bring the heat down to medium, add the remaining olive oil to the same pan and sauté the onion and leek until soft and glossy. Add the spring onions (scallions) and garlic, season with salt and pepper, then gently stir.

Return the meat to the pan and pour in the wine. Give it a few seconds, then pour in the warm stock. Cover with a well-fitting lid and simmer for 40–45 minutes until the meat feels tender and cooked.

Meanwhile, prepare the chard and lettuce. Place the leaves in a colander and gently wilt them by pouring boiling water over them.

Remove the lid from the cooking pan and add the vine leaves. Simmer, uncovered, for another 10 minutes, then add the chard, lettuce, dill and mint. Gently mix them into the simmering broth. Season with a little salt to taste. Cover again with the lid and let it simmer for another 10–15 minutes.

Ladle about 200ml (7fl oz) of cooking broth from the pot into a jug (pitcher) or cup. In a small bowl, mix the cornflour (cornstarch) into the lemon juice until it dissolves.

Separate the eggs. Whisk the egg whites to a light meringue (not too stiff). Whisk in the egg yolks until combined, then gradually start adding the lemon juice, whisking constantly. The result should be light and frothy. Slowly pour the hot broth into the egg and lemon mix, again whisking constantly (this way the temperature of the eggs increases enough to mix the sauce into the pot without curdling). Don't worry if there are pieces of onion or dill in there, it will all go back into the pot anyway. Pour it into the pot and gently shake it to mix in the sauce. Place back over a medium-low heat and bring to a simmer, then gently simmer over a very low heat for 2–3 minutes until the sauce thickens a bit and the flavours just combine.

Sweet and spicy quince mustard

This old recipe from Corfu, where it is known as *mostarda dolce* (sweet mustard), is a cousin of the Venetian *mostarda Veneta*. It is prepared with diced quince, simmered in wine and spices until soft enough to cream. The traditional recipe is also prepared with the addition of apples and pears, often with chopped candied citrus peel too, but I like to make it purely with quince and I keep it less sweet. The use of wine is essential here as it is an important flavour factor. I like to use a floral and fruity sweet white wine, like a Moscato from the island of Samos. That way the flavours are nicely balanced without the need to add sugar or apple to sweeten it. On Corfu, this delicate, aromatic mustard is traditionally served at Christmas alongside roasts. It's wonderful in sandwiches and on cheese or cold-cut platters.

MAKES 2 MEDIUM JARS

2½ tsp mustard seeds
1½ tbsp cider vinegar (or white wine vinegar)
850g (1lb 14oz) quinces (whole with skin)
½ lemon
600ml (20fl oz) sweet white wine (I use Moscato from Samos island)
¼ tsp ground cloves
1 tsp finely grated bergamot orange zest (if you can't get fresh bergamots, use zest from other aromatic citrus fruit or a combination; I often use pink grapefruit or half grapefruit, half orange)
2½ tsp hot mustard powder
Sea salt and white pepper

Crush the mustard seeds in a pestle and mortar, then place in a small bowl with the vinegar to infuse.

Peel, core and dice the quinces. Squeeze the lemon half over the quince to prevent browning and put in a medium saucepan. Pour in the wine and add the ground cloves, citrus zest and a pinch of salt; the wine should cover the quince. Place over a medium heat, bring to the boil, then reduce the heat to low. Gently simmer for about 30 minutes until the quince is very soft and easy to mash. The liquid should be absorbed by this point.

Transfer the quince to a blender or food processor. Add the mustard powder, along with the vinegar and crushed seeds and process until smooth. Season with salt and white pepper to taste. Store in sterilized jars in the refrigerator. If stored properly, it will keep well for about a year.

Fried sweet light-green peppers with vinegar

Here is a nice starter and a classic meze dish that is prepared all over Greece. The tradition of sharing food is very common in Greece, with the types of alcohol served alongside including ouzo, *tsipouro* or *tsikoudia* (also known as *raki*), wine and beer. Around the country, there are special restaurants dedicated to this way of eating and drinking, generally called *mezedopolia*, and, more specifically, there are also *ouzeri* and *tsipouradiko*, among others.

In this meze dish, sweet light green peppers are pan-fried in olive oil until soft and golden. The peppers are dressed in plenty of vinegar, either to enjoy straight away and warm, or to preserve and eat cold. If you wish to preserve them, let them cool down after frying, then store them in a glass container or jar with 2–3 sliced garlic cloves and enough vinegar to cover the peppers.

You can also replace the mild peppers with a spicy variety of chilli, or use a mix of different kinds of peppers, for an extra kick of flavour.

SERVES 4–6 AS PART OF A MEZE
6 long, sweet light green peppers
  (I try to choose relatively small ones)
Olive oil, for frying
2 garlic cloves, peeled and bashed
70ml (2½fl oz) white wine vinegar (or red, if you prefer)
Flaky sea salt

TO SERVE
Extra virgin olive oil, to drizzle
Finely grated lemon zest
½ tbsp chopped parsley
1 tbsp toasted pine nuts

Wash the peppers and dry them well using a dish towel. Pierce them all over with a toothpick or a fork.

Place a frying pan (use one with a lid), large enough to fit the peppers, over a medium heat. Add enough olive oil to cover the bottom of the pan by 5mm (¼ inch). Once hot, place the peppers and garlic cloves in the oil and reduce the heat to medium-low. Cover the pan with a lid and gently fry the peppers for about 10–15 minutes, turning them occasionally, until soft and golden all around.

Discard the garlic cloves, remove the pan from the heat and sprinkle the peppers with sea salt. If you wish to store them, first give them time to cool down a bit, then follow the instructions described in the recipe introduction.

If you are planning to serve them straight away, pour over the vinegar and let them marinate for at least 10–15 minutes.

Transfer to a platter, drizzle with a few drops of extra virgin olive oil, sprinkle with lemon zest, parsley and pine nuts, and serve.

Slow-cooked cockerel in wine, served over pasta

Cockerels are used in various recipes around Greece, as a result of the rural way of life: when roosters grow old and have no other purpose to serve on the farm, they are served as a feast. They are tastier than chicken and for that reason I highly recommend using them in stocks, soups and stews. Cockerel cooked in an aromatic tomato sauce with red wine is particularly popular. It is commonly served over pasta such as traditional *hylopites* (Greek noodles made with milk and eggs), thick spaghetti or bucatini. As cockerel meat can be tough, it requires gentle, slow cooking. Marinating the cockerel in wine is also recommended for more tender meat, and overall a tastier result.

I like to leave the skin and bones as they add lots of flavour to these kinds of slow-cooked dishes. If you prefer to make it with fillets, then make a strong-flavoured stock using the skin and bones. This recipe can be also made with chicken, in which case choose a good-quality, free-range chicken. As in most other cases where wine plays a central role in a recipe, both the type and quality are very important.

Serve this with *hylopites*, tagliatelle, pappardelle, spaghetti or bucatini, and sprinkle with grated cheese such as *kefalotyri*, dried *mizithra* or pecorino.

SERVES 4–6

1 cockerel (or free-range chicken), about 2kg (4lb 6oz), cut into 8 portions
1 sprig of basil, plus extra small or sliced leaves, to serve
1 small chilli (optional)
100ml (3½fl oz) olive oil
1 large onion, chopped
4 garlic cloves, chopped
1 large carrot, diced
500g (1lb 2oz) grated or chopped tomatoes (fresh or canned)
About 340ml (11½fl oz) hot chicken stock or water
2 tbsp tomato purée (paste) (double or triple concentration)
Sea salt and freshly ground black pepper

FOR THE MARINADE

300ml (10fl oz) dry red wine (I use a dry Mavrodaphne)
70ml (2½fl oz) sweet red wine (I use a sweet Mavrodaphne)
2 bay leaves
½ tbsp allspice berries
1 cinnamon stick
10 cloves

Season the cockerel pieces with salt and pepper and place in a large bowl. Add all the marinade ingredients, cover and leave to marinate in the refrigerator for 5–10 hours, or overnight.

Remove the cockerel pieces from the marinade, and strain and reserve the liquid and spices. Place the strained spices in a small pouch, made using a cheesecloth and string, along with the basil (cut it into smaller pieces to fit in the pouch) and the chilli, if using.

Place a large, wide cooking pot over a medium-high heat. Add the olive oil and brown the cockerel pieces, no more than three at a time to keep the oil temperature high. Place on a platter and set aside.

In the same cooking pot, using the same olive oil, sauté the onion until it softens. Add the garlic and carrot and sauté for 2–3 minutes. Return the cockerel pieces to the pot, pour in the strained marinade, add the spice pouch and reduce the heat to medium-low. Once the wine has reduced by half, add the tomatoes and enough stock or water to just cover the cockerel.

Season with salt and pepper to taste and reduce the heat to low. Cover and gently

simmer for 1–1½ hours or until the cockerel is fork-tender and falling off the bone. (If using chicken it will require a bit less time.)

At this point, mix in the tomato purée (paste) and gently simmer, partly covered, over a low heat for another 20 minutes until the sauce thickens. Adjust the seasoning, if necessary, discard the spice pouch, remove from the heat and let stand for 10 minutes before serving. Sprinkle with extra basil and serve with the pasta and cheese of your choice.

Soutzoukakia, meatballs with red wine

My son Apollo particularly loves this dish, and will happily eat it for several days in a row without tiring of it!

The name has Ottoman roots, deriving from the Turkish word *sucuk,* a spicy, fermented sausage. The Greeks of Anatolia, and particularly Smyrna (now Izmir), created this variation of the recipe. They kept the oblong shape of the *sucuk,* ditching the intestinal tissue and adding red wine to the mix, and serve it with a luscious tomato sauce that often has the addition of butter for extra richness and texture. The Greek version arrived in the early 1920s along with the Greek refugees from the coast of Turkey.

Some cooks, including my mother (who inherited this recipe from her grandmother), bake the meatballs along with potatoes and sliced tomatoes, but I must confess my preference is for the stovetop version with the sauce. I use olive oil and instead of a dry red wine, I use a sweet red wine, usually a Vinsanto from Santorini or Mavrodaphne from the Peloponnese (you can substitute these with a sweet Port, Madeira or any other sweet red wine of your choice). Should you prefer to avoid pan-frying, you can bake them in the oven or grill (broil) them instead, adding them to the sauce once they are cooked.

SERVES 4–6

130g (4½oz) stale bread (no crusts), chopped into pieces
300ml (10fl oz) red Vinsanto or Mavrodaphne wine
700g (1lb 9oz) minced (ground) beef (shoulder/chuck and blade if possible)
1 large egg
4–5 garlic cloves, minced
1 rounded tsp ground cumin
2 tbsp olive oil
2 tsp salt
1 tsp freshly ground black pepper
Sunflower oil, for frying
Mashed or fried potatoes or rice, to serve

FOR THE TOMATO SAUCE

1 tbsp olive oil
1 large garlic clove, finely chopped
2 bay leaves
1 tbsp tomato purée (paste)
2 tsp grape or fig molasses
120ml (4fl oz) red Vinsanto or Mavrodaphne wine, or sweet Port
900g (2lb) ripe tomatoes, skinned and pulsed or grated (or use chopped canned tomatoes)
1 tsp dried oregano
1 tbsp chopped parsley, plus extra to serve

Put the bread in a bowl, pour over the wine and soak for 10–15 minutes. Strain the bread (keep the wine) and shred it with your fingers.

In a large bowl, combine the beef, egg, garlic, cumin, shredded bread with any soaking wine, olive oil, salt and pepper. Knead thoroughly, cover and chill for about 1 hour. Shape the mixture into small, oblong meatballs (about 30) and set aside.

In a frying pan, heat enough sunflower oil for frying. Shallow-fry your meatballs for 2–3 minutes each side, until golden brown, then place on kitchen paper to drain.

For the tomato sauce, heat the olive oil in a large saucepan. Add the garlic and bay leaves and sauté for 1 minute. Next, add the tomato purée (paste) and molasses and stir. Follow with the wine, then add the grated tomatoes with all their juices and stir again. If the sauce is too dry, add a bit of water, but no more than half a wine glass. Simmer for about 15 minutes before adding the meatballs and oregano and continuing to simmer for another 10–15 minutes.

Add most of the parsley to the sauce. Serve the meatballs with mashed or fried potatoes, or with rice. Sprinkle with the remaining parsley and freshly ground black pepper.

Boubouristi, pan-fried snails with sea salt, rosemary and vinegar

Snails have been widely used in Hellenic cuisine since the Minoan times, and the ancient Greeks considered them a great delicacy and aphrodisiac. Aristotle designed a special tool to eat snails and Hippocrates used them for medicinal purposes, mostly to treat skin irritations or for skin rejuvenation. Snails are highly nutritious and a great source of protein; they are very low in fat and rich in vitamin A and minerals (such as iron, calcium and selenium), and high in omega-3 and -6, just like seafood. In times of war and hunger, snails were a 'free protein' and, combined with the seasonal edible weeds that grow abundantly in Greece, they provided people with much needed nutrition.

Snails are similar to shellfish; to consume them fresh, you must first make sure they are alive. Place them in a colander, in the sink, and wash them well with plenty of cold running water. They will start to move. Place the colander with the snails in a large bowl full of cold water. Let them sit like this for about 30–40 minutes. While you wait, cover them with something heavy or you will have to go snail hunting in your own kitchen! The ones that do not respond need to be discarded. Wash the live snails again thoroughly with cold water and they are ready to boil.

If you can't get fresh snails, you can still cook this dish – skipping the washing and boiling stages – using snail fillets from a jar. One last tip is that once you boil the snails, you can freeze and store them for future use.

Enjoy the snails with fresh bread and pair them with good red wine or *tsipouro.*

SERVES 4 AS A SHARING PLATE
1 tbsp sea salt
2 tbsp red wine vinegar
2 bay leaves
500g (1lb 2oz) live snails in their shell, cleaned and ready to cook
2 tbsp plain (all-purpose) flour
Enough coarse sea salt to cover the bottom of the pan
100ml (3½fl oz) olive oil
2 garlic cloves, peeled and bashed
1 tsp dried rosemary
2 sprigs of rosemary
100ml (3½fl oz) red wine vinegar

Fill a large pot that has a well-fitting lid with cold water. Bring to the boil and add the 1 tablespoon sea salt, vinegar and bay leaves. Throw in the prepared snails, cover, lower the heat and gently boil for 15–20 minutes. (Old-school, traditional cooks often throw dried fig leaves or fennel into the boiling water for aroma.) While the snails are boiling, skim off any froth formed on the surface using a slotted spoon. Drain the snails and let them stand to dry for a few minutes, then place on a tray, shell up, and dust with the flour.

Place a large frying pan over a medium-high heat and cover the base of the pan with a thin layer of coarse sea salt. Place each snail 'standing' on the salted pan. All the snails should fit in one layer, side by side. Give them 2–3 minutes to absorb the salt in the hot pan, then pour in the olive oil and add the garlic and dried and fresh rosemary. Fry for 4–5 minutes then pour in the vinegar and cook for another 1–2 minutes.

Serve in a slightly deep plate, along with the sauce from the pan.

Stuffed baked quince in a spiced brandy and rose syrup

In Greek mythology, the quince tree is dedicated to the goddess Aphrodite, who is often depicted holding its fruit – a symbol of love, beauty, fertility and devotion – in her right hand. This may be related to how quince has come to be considered a great aphrodisiac for women.

Baked quinces are a favourite winter treat and a great pairing with a cup of tea. I always use the seeds and skin when I cook quince – their high pectin content helps set the syrup or sauce. You can also keep the seeds and use them in other recipes that require thickening agents.

I often play with the syrup and have concluded that this one is my absolute favourite. It is elegant, with a wonderful aroma and flavour from the rose and the other spices used. Once the quinces are done, I strain the syrup and keep it in the refrigerator. You can use it in several ways – drizzled on cakes, pancakes, ice cream or yogurt.

SERVES 4

2 large quinces (each about 350–400g/
   12–14oz)
Juice of 1 lemon
300g (10½oz) brown cane sugar (fine)
50ml (2fl oz) Metaxa or brandy
1 tsp finely grated orange zest
130ml (4½fl oz) fresh orange juice
100ml (3½fl oz) warm water
1 cinnamon stick
½ vanilla pod (bean)
6–7 cloves
2 tbsp (about 15–18) small dried whole
   rosebuds (for tea) or rose petal tea

FOR THE STUFFING

½ tsp finely grated orange zest
30g (1oz) almonds, finely chopped
30g (1oz) walnuts, finely chopped
20g (¾oz) currants
1 tbsp brown sugar

Preheat the oven to 210°C/190°C fan/410°F/ gas mark 6½.

Wash the quinces and rub them to remove any fluff on the skin. Halve and core them, scooping out the seeds and core and creating a small hole in their centre, big enough to stuff. Reserve the seeds. Brush the cut sides of the quinces with some of the lemon juice to prevent them from browning.

Place the quince halves cut side down in a medium, deep baking dish.

In a medium bowl, combine the sugar, Metaxa or brandy, remaining lemon juice, orange zest and juice, and water. Mix well with a spoon and pour into the baking dish. Add the cinnamon stick, vanilla pod (bean), cloves, rosebuds and reserved quince seeds.

Bake on a low oven shelf for 30–40 minutes or until the quinces soften.

Meanwhile, add all the stuffing ingredients to a bowl, mix well to combine and set aside.

Once the quinces are ready, remove them from the oven and carefully flip them cut side up.

Stuff each with about 2 teaspoons of the filling (depending on the size of the hole). Spoon some of the hot syrup from the baking dish over the quinces and stuffing, avoiding any seeds or spices (use a small sieve when you do this).

Return the quinces to the oven for 20 minutes until they turn nice and golden. Transfer to a platter and carefully strain the syrup. The quince is lovely served on its own, simply drizzled with the syrup. I recommend you also try it with a fresh white, creamy cheese like a Greek *anthotyro* or an Italian ricotta, or simply a scoop of yogurt or ice cream drizzled with this wonderful syrup.

Index

Suppliers

These days you can find pretty much any ingredient online and so here I've collated a list of reputable suppliers.

UK

Agora Greek delicacies
agoragreekdelicacies.co.uk

Greek Market
greekmarket.co.uk

Bakalikon
bakalikon.co.uk

Hellenic Grocery
hellenicgrocery.co.uk

Maltby and Greek
maltbyandgreek.com

Odysea
odysea.com

Taste Greece
tastegreece.co.uk

Oliveology
oliveology.co.uk

Oh my Greek
ohmygreek.co.uk

The Greek deli
thegreekdeli.com

Ergon Deli
ergonfoods.com

Isle of Olive
isleofolive.co.uk

Athenian Grocery
atheniangrocery.co.uk

Ormos Foodhall
greekselect.com

Kokoraki Deli
kokorakideli.com

USA

Yoleni's
yolenis.com

Optima Foods
optimafoods.com

Greek Food Emporium
greekfoodemporiumny.com

Prima Foods
primafoodsinc.com

Recipiada
Recipiada.com

Mediterranean Foods
Mediterraneanfoodsny.com

Acknowledgements

I want to thank every single person who openheartedly helped and supported the making of this book. There are so many people to thank: friends and co-workers, past and present.

I want to thank my family for providing the right foundations in my upbringing and education and particularly my mother, Tesi, for showing her endless love and trust; my son Apollo, who has been tasting and judging my recipes in this book with the maturity and expertise of a connoisseur and bearing with my non-stop writing!

Thank you, Diane Kochilas, for your loving support and friendship, and for all the knowledge and expertise I have gained through our work together over the past years. It's been invaluable.

I want to thank Tina for making me believe in this project and giving me the push to actually go for it. A big thanks to Foteini and to Mrs. Marianna Nikolaou, who provided information about certain recipes, to Andreas the beekeeper on Tinos and Christos the fisherman on Aegina, to the inspiring Culinary Backstreets family around the world, and to George for reading and advising and for providing his lovely house on Tinos for some of the shooting.

A huge thanks to all the Quadrille team and particularly Céline for believing in this, and Stacey and Claire for collaborating in such good spirit, for being patient, and for showing me so much trust.

Manos, I am eternally grateful for your amazing work, the stunning photos, your patience, for your personal time and touch, for the extra work you put into this (much more than what I anticipated), and, of course, for the great fun we had throughout.

I particularly want to thank Carly Martin because without her contribution this book wouldn't be what it is. I thank her for her true friendship above all and the work and help she has generously offered for the conception and making of the book; always by my side like a wise sister, advising me, organizing me, and inspiring me, trying out my recipes and bearing with my endless dilemmas and early morning texting!

Managing Director Sarah Lavelle
Senior Commissioning Editor Céline Hughes
Commissioning Editor Stacey Cleworth
Art Direction and Design Claire Rochford
Typesetting Gemma Hayden
Photographer Manos Chatzikonstantis
Head of Production Stephen Lang
Production Controller Gary Hayes

Published in 2023 by Quadrille
an imprint of Hardie Grant Publishing

Quadrille
52–54 Southwark Street
London SE1 1UN
quadrille.com

ISBN 9781787138544

Printed in China